THE HANDWRITING
OF
ENGLISH DOCUMENTS

THE HANDWRITING
OF
ENGLISH DOCUMENTS

by

L. C. HECTOR, M.A.

An Assistant Keeper of the Public Records ;
Lecturer in Palaeography, University College, London

I cannot carry my Respect for Antiquity so far as not to
recollect that the direct Purpose, and therefore the first
Merit, of writing, is to be easily read by all.
JOHN RICKMAN, Clerk Assistant of the House
of Commons, 3 March 1836

LONDON
EDWARD ARNOLD (PUBLISHERS) LTD

Printed in Great Britain by Butler and Tanner Ltd., Frome and London

PREFACE

In my twenty-seven years at the Public Record Office there have been very few of my colleagues who have not contributed in some way to my education in the matters discussed in these pages. Both to my seniors, wise, patient, and infinitely generous with their help and counsel, and to my juniors, for their friendly purveyance of discoveries of all kinds, I owe a debt of gratitude which I am glad to have this opportunity of acknowledging. In preparing this book I have incurred additional obligations, especially to my friends Mr. H. C. Johnson and Mr. D. B. Wardle, not only for signal services rendered but also for their interest and encouragement, and to Mr. R. E. Latham, Mr. C. A. F. Meekings, and Mr. E. K. Timings, each of whom has supplied to me information of great value for my purposes.

Outside the Record Office I have profited from the kindness of Mr. M. F. Bond, who drew my attention to an interesting Report by a House of Lords Committee of 1836, and Mr. J. H. P. Pafford, who read the book in draft and made a number of helpful suggestions, most of which have been gratefully adopted.

For permission to use the photographs reproduced in the plates I am indebted as follows :

Plate I (a) and (b)	The Trustees of the British Museum
Plate I (c), Plates II–VI, Plate VII (a) and (c), Plates VIII–XXIV, XXVI–XXXI .	The Deputy Keeper of the Records
Plate VII (b).	The Controller of Her Majesty's Stationery Office
Plate XXV	The Rev. Canon J. S. Purvis, Director of the Borthwick Institute, York
Plate XXXII	The Very Rev. the Dean of York

March 1958   L. C. H.

CONTENTS

LIST OF PLATES

(pp. 65–96)

9

INTRODUCTION

The chief object of this book is to moderate as far as possible the difficulties of reading presented by the hands written in England for administrative, legal or business purposes during the past eight or nine centuries. This period, chosen primarily because the overwhelming majority of surviving English manuscript archives fall within its chronological limits, has the accidental advantage of beginning at a time when the letter-forms in use make comparatively easy reading for a modern eye, and is long enough to enable the development of the later hands to be seen in something like perspective.

Some of the subjects which may properly claim attention in a work such as this are suggested by the catalogue of his early difficulties recited by an 18th-century student of manuscript records :

> There is something indeed highly discouraging and irksome in the first outset of an attempt of this kind. The strange uncouth hand in which many of the ancient manuscripts are wrote, the precise similarity of shape in which several letters of the alphabet are struck, the arbitrary substitution of a few letters with circumflexes and characters to signify whole words, the parchment or paper changed, and the ink mouldered away . . . all these circumstances make it comparatively as difficult to become a perfect master of the hand as it would be to acquire a new language.[1]

There was a time, not long past, when these ' circumstances ' would have been said to be the province, almost the whole province, of palaeography. Until late in the 19th century few scholars would have questioned the accuracy or the completeness of Littré's only definition of *paléographie* as ' art de déchiffrer les écritures anciennes, et, particulièrement, les manuscrits grecs et latins, les chartes et diplômes du moyen âge, etc.'. The special mention of charters and diplomas serves as a reminder of the origin of palaeography as a branch of diplomatic, the science of documentary criticism, in which its main function had been to enable the student to read the handwritings of the past by teaching him to identify their letter-forms and to expand their abbreviations.

But today most scholars claiming to be called palaeographers would consider this a very restricted and old-fashioned view of the scope and functions of their subject, which, as now pursued, has little but its name in common with that defined by Littré. As the 19th century drew to a close palaeographers everywhere took advantage of technical advances in the field of photography to apply comparative methods to their study of the external features of manuscripts. Examination of the disciplined work of the book-scribe revealed that there were rules of calligraphy, scribal practices and conventions, and styles of decoration, which were associated with specific places and periods of origin, so that it was possible to set up strictly palaeographical criteria of date and provenance for literary and liturgical texts. The preoccupation with material of this kind (to the criticism of which

---

[1] Rev. John Bree : *A Cursory Sketch . . . of this Kingdom during the 14th century, etc.* (1791), Introduction, p. v. It is reassuring to know that Bree felt himself compensated for his efforts : ' for there is, in my opinion, in the composition of those early ages . . . a chaste, nervous simplicity and definite, correct precision that is strikingly pleasing and beautiful ' (*Ibid.*, p. vi).

palaeography has a unique contribution to make) has persisted ; and nowadays the palaeo-grapher is apt either to exclude altogether from his consideration the hands written in archives or to admit them only as a possible influence on the development of the literary hands. His interest is in such questions as the activity and influence of schools of hand-writing and illumination, the territorial distribution of styles, and the successive stages in the transmission of texts.

Many of the questions he has equipped himself to answer do not arise at all in the documents with which this book is concerned ; and in any attempt to apply his new-found methods of study he is gravely handicapped here by the fact that most of the hands written in English archives do not lend themselves to precise and confident classification by date and provenance. The self-conscious set hands which begin to appear in the 15th century are associated not with schools of handwriting in the cultural or local sense but with professional *milieux* and departments of administration ; they are seldom seen except as the conventionally obligatory vehicles for formal documents of specific kinds. Outside such formal contexts the business hands of any one period may exhibit all the variety of which individualism is capable,[1] and every document may be expected to illustrate in some degree the idiosyncrasies of its writer. For documents to be identifiable as the work of individuals may on occasion be useful to the student, but the capacity to recognise a familiar handwriting is hardly palaeography.

It is undeniable, of course, that most of even the free hands of the same approximate date have a certain resemblance to one another, often vague and difficult to define, but none the less perceptible ; and it is certainly possible for the experienced student of English archives to formulate a composite mental picture of what, for practical purposes, he can regard as an archive hand 'typical' of this or that period in England. It does not matter that for the period in question actual written examples precisely simulating this notional 'type' may be rarer than those which vary in some important detail from it : the student with sufficient experience does come to carry in his eye something like a set of standards for application to the documents he examines.

The same experience, however, will have taught him how seldom there is any real occasion for these standards to be critically applied. As a rule, English archives are expressly dated ; and though there are important exceptions to the rule the nature of archives is such that the best evidence of a document's date and of the circumstances of its writing is almost certain to be internal, whether such evidence is historical (and verified by independently ascertained facts about the people, the events, or the administrative processes mentioned) or diplomatic (and afforded by the structure and phraseology of the text itself). Until the reign of Richard I few English royal charters bore any date of time, and it was not until a further century had passed that it became usual for private deeds to include a dating clause. Often the earliest extant text of an ancient charter, royal or private, is a copy, written centuries after the original, in the cartulary of a religious house or in the rolls of a royal court. Yet for the purpose of judgements about date or genuine-ness such a transcript is little less valuable than the sealed engrossment would have been, had it survived.

[1] For a striking demonstration of the differences possible between 'free' hands of the same date and from the same locality, see Hilary Jenkinson : *Palaeography and the Practical Study of Court Hand* (Cambridge, 1915).

The only archive material that is dated by its handwriting is that to which no other criterion can be applied. For the most part it will be found to be of minor importance, consisting of such accretions to earlier texts as annotations, corrections, dockets and endorsements, with, perhaps, an occasional uninformative fragment or a whole document lacking all context. The needs of scholarship are usually met if the date allotted to such material on the evidence of its handwriting can be taken to be correct to within fifty years, which by the wise student of archive hands is reckoned to be close palaeographical dating. He knows that a habit of being proved spectacularly right in such matters is no protection against being on occasion spectacularly wrong, when there is nothing to show whether he is dealing with the work of a member of the *avant-garde* or with that of an elderly clerk clinging to the style of his first youth. A certain diffidence, indeed, runs all through the applications of palaeography to the criticism of archives : the role of the palaeographer is usually to support, sometimes to anticipate, virtually never to challenge, conclusions based on internal evidence.

The handwritings of English archives seldom need, then, to be considered except in their primary function of a medium of communication—something to be read. Bree's eloquent complaints suggest that at times the task of reading them may be formidable enough ; and it must be admitted that so far as legibility is a matter of consistent and instantly recognised letter-forms the business hands of any period are likely to be more difficult to read than the literary hands contemporary with them. In practice it will be found that the difficulties are offset by other considerations and that a diversity of hands is often compensated by a certain uniformity of matter and style. Routine procedures inevitably produce routine documents. When once a satisfactory way of saying something has been devised it is not usual for men of business to seek gratuitously for new ways of expressing it. For the administrator the standardised formula has the double advantage of consistently presenting the same sort of information in the same way and of enabling much of the mechanical labour of writing to be delegated to humbler workers,[1] competent to copy but not to draft. The formulary, or collection of precedents, must have been in extensive use in England long before the 13th century, when the earliest examples we have were compiled.[2] Some formulae acquired a special status or value from having been the subject of judicial interpretation : the construction which the courts were known to put upon a phrase gave it a precision and authority which no drafter could afford to ignore.[3] Sometimes the forms and phraseology of whole documents are prescribed by royal or other authority, or by statute.[4] The influences at work to determine documentary form are part of the subject-matter of diplomatic, which seeks to construct, from external evidence and from the careful collation of documents similar in nature,

[1] The earliest surviving piece of English printing is a form—an indulgence issued on 13 December 1476 by Abbot Sant of Abingdon (P.R.O. Exchequer K.R. Eccl. Docts. 6/56).

[2] Cf. Spelman on the composition of the private charter : ' some Monk or Priest near the Time of the Conquest devised certain Classick Forms of explaining the Thing granted and the Appurtenants by exquisite Words and Phrases, which were much in Request '—*Reliquiae Spelmanniae* (1723), Part II, p. 246.

[3] A famous decision of the Court of Wards (in Tyrrell's Case, 1557) permanently added five words to the conveyance in trust.

[4] The form of the writ *de etate probanda* is laid down in the Close Roll for 7 Edward I (*Calendar of Close Rolls, 1272–79*, pp. 548–9) and that for the royal confirmation of charters (1285) is printed in *Statutes of the Realm*, I, pp. 104–5.

a system of doctrines about the form which a given document can be expected to take at a given date. These doctrines supply the canons of criticism by which date, provenance and genuineness may be determined; but clearly they may be of great service to the student who aspires to no more than accurate reading. If, having read the beginning of a phrase, he knows how it is likely to continue and end, his progress is bound to be easier; his mind will lead his eye. There is some truth in the paradox that legibility in a manuscript document consists chiefly in the reader's prior knowledge of what it contains. Certainly the most difficult documents to read are by no means necessarily those in the most outlandish hands: they are far more likely to be those which are cast in a form outside the reader's experience.

CHAPTER I

THE EQUIPMENT OF THE WRITERS

1

Writing Surfaces

The design and development of a manuscript alphabet are at all times directly influenced by the instruments and materials generally used for writing it. In the period covered by this book there are very few English archives of any importance that are not written in ink on parchment or paper. The properties of these materials and the ways in which writers handled them may bear from time to time on questions of interpretation.

The standard writing surface of medieval England for all purposes was provided by parchment, prepared from the skins of animals, of which the most usual were the sheep[1] and the goat. Vellum, a similar product, is strictly ' veal-parchment ', from the skins of calves, but the term is commonly applied also to parchment prepared from the skins of lambs and kids. An especially fine variety, known as ' abortive ' or ' uterine ' vellum and normally used only for the more sumptuous literary and liturgical manuscripts, was (or was said to be) made from the skins of stillborn and unborn calves, kids and lambs. The medieval parchment-maker soaked, scraped and rubbed the animal-skins in a series of processes,[2] of which the effect was to remove the hair or wool and to reduce the thickness by about half, before they were stretched on hoop-shaped frames to dry. The preparation of the parchment for writing was completed by the scribe, who smoothed its surface with pumice or even with a razor or a small plane. If the page was to be ruled he pricked the margin of his parchment at equal vertical intervals with an awl [3] to provide points of departure for the horizontal rulings, which might be lines drawn with a plummet (a small pointed piece of lead) or shallow furrows made with a blunt stylus. For ' boning ' or restoring the writing-surface after he had erased erroneous written matter with his knife he used a boar's tusk.[4]

Well-made parchment is thin, smooth and white, the whiteness often helped out by the pulverised chalk with which the surface was rubbed. Traces of this chalk can sometimes be seen on poor-quality parchments, which often present also an appearance of

---

[1] In the 12th-century Exchequer care was taken that the Pipe Rolls (the principal record of the sovereign's dealings with his debtors) should be of sheep-parchment, ' from which it is not easy to erase matter without leaving a conspicuous blemish '. See Charles Johnson (ed.) : *Dialogus de Scaccario* (Edinburgh, 1950), p. 35.

[2] The method of manufacture is discussed in D. V. Thompson : *Materials of Mediaeval Painting* (1936), pp. 24 ff.

[3] There seems to be no certain evidence of the use of a toothed wheel for this purpose. See L. W. Jones : ' Pricking Manuscripts ', in *Speculum*, Vol. XXI (1946), pp. 389–403.

[4] This account of the equipment of a medieval scribe is based on a passage in Caius College, Cambridge, MS. 385, p. 58, quoted and discussed in C. H. Haskins : *Studies in the History of Mediaeval Science* (Cambridge, Mass., 1924), p. 361.

greasiness or semi-transparency.   In almost all parchment there is a conspicuous difference in colour and texture between the two sides, the flesh side being whiter and somewhat smoother than the hair side, which may well be dark enough to be called brown.   Medieval directions to the reader sometimes distinguish between the contrasting sides : a 14th-century Customs Account[1] has a list of its own contents distributed into those which are *ex parte alba* (' on the light side ') and *ex parte nigra* (' on the dark side '), and in an Eyre Roll[2] of 1235 there occur the phrases *videatis in carne* (a reference-back from the hair side) and *respice in rotulo sequenti versus carnem.*

Attacks by warble-flies on the living animal, and accidental nicks made in the skin before the stretching and drying, produce in the finished parchment round or elliptical holes of distinctive appearance, with firm clean edges.   Parchment so holed was often used, doubtless for reasons of economy.   The medieval scribe whose progress brought him to the left-hand edge of a hole simply continued his writing on the farther side of it ; so that the presence of one of these ' original ' holes in a medieval parchment document does not imply, for the reader, the loss of any written matter.   From the 16th century, however, writers called upon to use holed parchment often covered the hole by pasting a patch on to the hair side and wrote over the patch.[3]

By the time paper appeared in England as an alternative writing material, the use of parchment had already come to be regarded as almost obligatory for certain kinds of documents.[4]   Many medieval series of records, particularly in the archives of the central government, continued without a break into the modern period, and for such records the traditional medieval material was retained.   The coming of the Tudors introduced considerable changes and innovations in the methods of business and administration.   New offices and new procedures produced new classes of records, for which paper was the normal vehicle.   It would not be an over-simplification to say that the consistent use of parchment for any purpose after the 15th century points to a survival of, or an analogy with, medieval practice and tradition, and that where there was no such tradition paper was used as a matter of course.   Thus the long series of Chancery enrolments, the Plea Rolls of the courts of common law, the written pleadings filed in the Chancery, and formal deeds and sealed instruments generally, are typical of the classes for which parchment was retained until the 19th century or even later.   The prestige attaching to parchment was obliquely recognised in 1853 by the introduction of ' japan vellum ' or ' vegetable parchment ', prepared by treating unsized paper successively with dilute sulphuric acid, water, and ammonia.

---

[1] Exchequer L.T.R. Enrolled Accounts (Customs), No. 13.

[2] Assize Rolls, etc., No. 80, mm. 14*d* and 21*d*.

[3] For a skilfully applied 17th-century example, see Chan. Proc. before 1714, Reynardson, 404/158 : Biddulph *v.* Grosvenor.

[4] The fact that a sealed instrument was of paper was thought worth remarking in 1384 in a record not as a rule lavish of irrelevant detail (C.P. Plea Roll, Trin. 8 Ric. II, rot. 348).

2

Paper

Occasional paper documents were reaching England from abroad as early as the reign of Henry III ; and after 1300 the new material rapidly became familiar to Englishmen who had dealings with the south-west of France, one of the first European centres, outside Spain, of its manufacture. During the 14th century paper was gradually taken into use in England for the humbler kinds of documents ; and by the end of the century paper is almost as likely as parchment to be the material chosen for household accounts. From this time forward the comparative cheapness of paper ensured its being preferred for less formal documents (in which there was an ever-increasing preponderance of correspondence and memoranda of all kinds) and for the newer purposes generally.[1] In view of this great and growing demand it is odd that it was not until late in the 17th century that the manufacture of paper was firmly established in this country and that up till then almost all the paper used here by the printer and by an increasing class of literates had to be imported. On watermarks as evidence of the provenance and the date of manufacture of paper there is a considerable body of published literature, headed by C. M. Briquet : *Les Filigranes* (Geneva, 1907), in four volumes.

3

Formats

English paper documents have almost all survived to us in formats with which the modern reader is already familiar, but some of the conventions governing the use of parchment are perhaps worth mention. In sealed parchment documents, such as charters, deeds and writs, the text is confined to the flesh side, and only endorsements are to be found on the hair side. Long texts (common from the 16th century onwards) are continued on the flesh sides of further skins, secured to the first by the seal-cords passing through the lower margins. Parchment rolls, a distinctively English format for records, are of two kinds, the first associated with the royal Chancery and the second with the Exchequer and the courts of common law. The practice in the Chancery, imitated from time to time outside it,[2] has always been to form the roll by sewing together, head to tail, oblong sheets of parchment (known as ' membranes ') and rolling them continuously so as to compose a cylinder. The inner surface of the membranes (the flesh side of the parchment) is known as the face of the roll, the outer (the hair side) as the back or ' dorse '.[3] The Chancery-type

---

[1] The price-tables printed in Sir William [now Lord] Beveridge and others : *Prices and Wages in England*, Vol. I (1939), pp. 85–7, show that between 1426 and 1541 the price paid by Winchester College for the dearer of two qualities (or two sizes) of paper remained remarkably steady at 5*s.* a ream of 20 quires. During this time the price paid for a dozen skins of parchment was seldom less than 2*s.* (average 2*s.* 7½*d.*). In the period 1561 to 1582, while the paper was being bought for 6*s.* 8*d.* a ream, the cost of a dozen skins of parchment fluctuated between 3*s.* 4*d.* and 6*s.*, averaging 4*s.* 5*d.*

[2] For example, in the earliest registers at York and Lincoln.

[3] In references, ' m. 7 ' means the face of membrane 7, and ' m. 7*d* ' its dorse.

H.E.D.—B

roll does not lend itself to quick reference : to consult the membrane at the centre of the cylinder it is necessary to unwind the whole roll (consisting of perhaps fifty membranes, each two feet long) and to wind it all back afterwards.   In the Exchequer and the courts of common law the roll was made up by piling the component sheets of parchment (here themselves described individually as rolls or *rotuli*) all flesh side uppermost, and securing them by cords passing through the heads, the lower ends being left free, so that quick reference is comparatively easy.   In the parchment book, bound after writing, care was taken that at whatever point the volume was opened there should not be a contrast between facing pages but that both should be flesh side or both hair side throughout the volume. To effect this a typical quire (*quaternio*) of four doubled sheets (*bifolia*), giving eight leaves (*folia*) or sixteen pages, would be folded and arranged as in the figure.

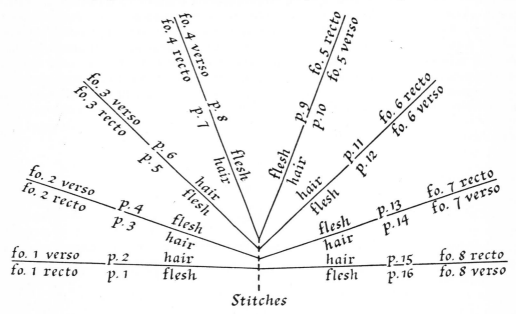

4

Pens

Metal pens faithfully imitating those made from quills were known to high antiquity ; and 18th-century sources[1] describe and illustrate a metal fountain-pen of some complexity of design.   But until the 19th century there was no really acceptable substitute for the quill pen.   The quills were ordinarily those of geese or swans, but for specially small or fine work crow-quills were used.   In the early 19th century the engrossing hand[2] was written with a wide-nibbed turkey-quill, which bit deep into the parchment and made it

---

[1] *Owen's Dictionary of Arts and Sciences* (2nd edn., 1764), Vol. III, p. 2421 and Plate CXCVI.
[2] See p. 64 and Plate XXXI below.

easy to lay on the quantity of ink which was deemed to confer superior ' durability ' on the hand.[1]   For this hand, and, indeed, for most of the hands discussed in this book, the quill was cut to an oblique edge, so that as long as the pen was held naturally and at a constant angle to the writing-surface the strokes it made were thick or thin according to the angle they made with this edge.   For the round hand of the 18th and 19th centuries[2] the goose-quill was cut to a symmetrically tapered fine point, which needed frequent ' mending ' (that is, re-cutting) by the writer.   The tendency of all quill pens to wear and soften quickly in use was their greatest defect[3] and presented to early 19th-century inventors a challenge which was met by such expedients as gilding the quills chemically, lapping their tips with thin sheet gold, incorporating in them minute fragments of diamond, ruby or other hard and non-corroding substances, and replacing quills by horn or tortoiseshell similarly rein-forced.   The problem was ultimately solved (or rather evaded) when Perry in 1830 and Gillott in 1831 introduced fine steel pens flexible enough to compete successfully with the quill as a means of writing round hand.   With these metal pens variations in thickness could be achieved only by conscious variation in the pressure applied ; and since heavy pressure could be applied only when the pen was drawn towards the writer's hand, the characteristic Victorian contrast was between thin up-strokes and thick down-strokes : a monotonous and mechanical alternation of pressure and release was imported into the physical act of writing and all the letters of the alphabet tended to be dragged into the shape best adapted to the rhythm.

5

Inks

In 1836, however, criticism of the steel pen rested on other grounds :

Within the last two or three years steel pens have come into general use, especially among the law stationers ; for the commodious activity of these pens, very liquid ink, and therefore pale ink, is almost indispensable, and when applied on glazed paper (introduced for the same purpose), and speedily dried on blotting paper, the characters nearly disappear ; yet so prevalent, I may add so profitable to the manufacturer, is this feeble ink that no good black ink can now be procured . . .[4]

Black inks of all periods can be divided into two classes, those which contain iron salts and those which do not.   Until about 1500 the standard black ink used in England belonged to the first class : medieval recipes for making ink (which are not uncommon) call for galls, copperas or vitriol, and gum.   (See Plate XII (a).)   The galls are the small spherical swellings, often called oak-apples, produced on the twigs of the oak-tree by the activities of the parasitic gall-fly ; ' copperas ' and ' vitriol ' are synonymous terms for what the

[1] House of Lords Sessional Papers, 1836, IX. 407.

[2] See p. 60 below.

[3] Bramah, who patented a process for economising quills, referred to them in 1809 as ' the present expensive article ' (Close Roll, 49 Geo. III, Part 24, No. 3).

[4] House of Lords Sessional Papers, 1836, IX. 407.

modern chemist calls proto-sulphate of iron. The ingredients were put together and stirred frequently over a period of two or three weeks, after which, suitably diluted with water, the ink was ready for use. The combination of the iron salt with the gallic or tannic acid contained in the galls produces a purplish-black compound which in normal conditions grows even darker with age. The great durability of iron inks earned for them their medieval name of *incausta* (derived from the Greek ἐγκαίω, ' burn in ') because the way in which they integrated themselves with the surface to which they were applied was conceived as a figurative ' burning in '. When writing in one of these inks has faded it can often be made legible if traces of the iron compound are still present in the surface of the parchment or paper. Until fairly recently chemical reagents (solutions of gallic acid or ammonium sulphide were the commonest) were applied to ' bring up ' these traces, though it had long been known that, unless it was well diluted, gallic acid in the course of time imparted an ineradicable stain and made illegibility total and permanent. The use of these reagents is nowadays strongly deprecated and recourse is rather had to ultra-violet or infra-red rays as an aid to reading faded and ' blind ' documents. Ultra-violet light can be used either for immediate visual examination or for making a photograph : its property is to cause fluorescence, a visible glow, in certain organic substances. Metals and metallic compounds impede this fluorescence, so that under ultra-violet light in a darkened room any traces of iron ink present in the surface of a faded document will stand out black against a luminous background. A document treated in the past with gallic acid will not fluoresce. Infra-red rays make no directly visible difference to the legibility of faded documents, but they may enable legible photographs to be made of matter obliterated by ink, pigment, or even a layer of paper.[1]

Of black inks not containing iron the commonest until a fairly late date were suspensions of carbon in gum-water. The carbon, usually obtained in the form of lamp-black, provided an immediate and dense black which commended itself especially to the writers of ornamental headings. But these inks lacked the ingredients by which modern Indian ink is rendered waterproof ; and even in favourable conditions the durability of writing in them is uncertain. The carbon does not integrate itself with the writing-surface, to which it is bound only by the gum ; on the failure of the gum it is apt to crack off. When this has happened the best the reader can hope for is that the document as a whole became dirty before the loss of the ink, so that the surfaces protected by the ink may preserve the writing, somewhat precariously, in the form of ' white on grey '. Pure carbon inks were not used for documents intended to have any legal validity, but from the 15th century onwards carbon was occasionally added to iron inks to achieve a more intense or more immediate blackness than was possible with unadulterated iron inks.

[1] See the *Journal* of the Royal Society of Arts, 3 February 1933, p. 271.

CHAPTER II

THE EQUIPMENT OF THE READER

1

Languages

Opinions differ about the value of a formal training in palaeography to the student who wishes to use manuscript sources. Sir Percy Winfield thought that such a training was wholly unnecessary,[1] Professor Charles Langlois that it was almost indispensable ;[2] but even between these two conflicting authorities there is no disagreement about the student's need to know the languages in which his manuscripts are written.

There is irony in the circumstance that it took the revival of classical learning to establish the modern view that Latin is a dead language. Save that it was nobody's mother tongue and that it found its chief employment in writing, Latin at the time of the Norman conquest of England showed every sign of life and even of growth. As the language of the Western Church it was common ground to the ' clerks ', English and Norman, from whom the Conqueror and his successors recruited their civil service, and was thus a peculiarly suitable medium for official records ; but it might well have been chosen on its merits for the task of providing formal written expression for all the processes of English business and administration, a task which it discharged virtually alone for about two hundred years.

During this period the language spoken by the governing classes of society and in the oral proceedings of English courts of law was the kind of French now usually called Anglo-Norman. Towards the end of the 13th century, when developments in administration began to produce documents of a new and less ceremonious character, this French, hitherto very sparsely represented in archives, was preferred to Latin for such documents and for a great deal of the material, such as correspondence, which called for original composition. This points less, perhaps, to the dominance in England of the Anglo-Norman vernacular than to the contemporary status of French as a language read by literates whose literacy did not, or did not always, extend to Latin. But even in the 14th century, when documents in Anglo-Norman are at their most numerous, they form only a very small fraction of the whole mass of contemporary English archives.[3] A statute of 1362[4] provided that

---

[1] *Chief Sources of English Legal History* (Cambridge, 1925), p. 18 : ' where it is necessary to read a manuscript, it is quite possible to do this without the slightest training in palaeography '.

[2] *Introduction to the Study of History* (with Charles Seignobos) (Eng. trans. 1898), p. 49 : ' Scholars who have received no regular palaeographical initiation can almost always be recognised by the gross errors which they commit from time to time in deciphering.'

[3] The approximate proportion of Latin to Anglo-Norman writing in this century is put by S. Harrison Thomson at a thousand to one (' The Criteria of Latin Palaeography in the Study of Anglo-Norman Documents ', *Romanic Review*, April 1938).

[4] 36 Edw. III, st. 1, c. 15.

21

' because the French tongue is much unknown in the realm ' pleas in the royal and other courts should be debated in English and entered and enrolled in Latin.   In so far as Latin was already, and always had been, the language of the official records, one of these provisions was otiose.   The other was for immediate practical purposes ineffective, since French continued to be the distinctive professional idiom of the common law.   Long after it had died out of spoken use everywhere else in England it remained the language of oral argument in court and of the Year Books in which such argument was reported.[1]   But outside the legal profession the use of Anglo-Norman declined steadily after 1400 ; and when, in 1487, it ceased to be the language employed in framing the operative parts of Parliamentary statutes it lost its last important function and survived only in a few traditional formulae like *Le Roy le veult*.

In 1422 the London brewers had decided that henceforward they would keep their records in English because by the King's use of it in his letters missive (that is, his informal correspondence) and in his other personal business ' their mother tongue was beginning to gain lustre ' and because there were many of their craft who read and wrote English but did not understand Latin or French.[2]   In the course of the 15th century English ousted Anglo-Norman from the archive contexts with which it had been associated ; and it was English which became the vehicle for almost all the documentary types resulting from Tudor innovations.   Elsewhere Latin remained strongly entrenched in the territory which had never been surrendered to Anglo-Norman ; and by 1500 the domestic field was divided, roughly speaking, between Latin for the traditional formal document and English for the new and less formal one.

The next century and a half witnessed the slow decline of Latin as a language for English archives.   The classes of documents for which Latin was used during this period are both numerous and important : they embrace, for example, many of the deeds executed by private parties, most of the sealed instruments issuing from the royal and the palatinate Chanceries, and all the records of the courts of common law.   But the medieval idiom in which these documents were couched had been abandoned by academic Latinists at the Renaissance and now survived only as part of the stock in trade of a few isolated professional groups.   There was never any prospect of its being generally replaced or in any significant sense supplemented in records by the Latin of the humanists.   Special considerations might lead to the employment of Camden in 1611 to compose for the patent of baronetcy a piece of pure public-orator prose ; but for the most part it was as if Latin needed medieval precedents and models in order to be used at all.   The extent to which it was being written at the beginning of the Interregnum can be gauged from an Act of November 1650, which was clearly meant to put an end to the use of Latin in domestic records.   From 1 January 1651 ' all writs, proces and returns thereof, pleadings, rules, orders, indictments, inquisitions, certificates, all patents, commissions, records, judgements, statutes, recognizances, rolls, entries, and proceedings of courts leet, courts baron and customary courts ' were to be ' in English and not in Latin, French, or any other language ', and were to be written ' in an ordinary, usual and legible hand and character and not

---

[1] Sir John Cavendish, Chief Justice of the King's Bench, confesses in his will, dated 1381, that he and his friends were more at home with French than with Latin (*Archaeologia*, XI, p. 55).

[2] R. W. Chambers and M. Daunt : *London English* (Oxford, 1931), pp. 16 and 139.

in any hand commonly called court hand '.[1] For the next nine years, therefore, the official use of Latin was confined to the purposes of international communication.

On the restoration of the monarchy in 1660 all the legislation of the Interregnum was abrogated ; and for wholly irrelevant political reasons Latin and the court hands returned to the contexts from which they had been expelled. But by 1731 the case for their abolition was again being debated on its merits. In that year a Bill was introduced which repeated the provisions of the Commonwealth Act with the minor elaboration that the records specified were to be written in ' such a common legible hand and character as the Acts of Parliament are usually engrossed in . . . and not in any hand commonly called court hand, and in words at length and not abbreviated '. These changes were to take effect in 1733. Against the Bill it was argued that it would make the existing records unintelligible to a new generation.

> To this it was answer'd by the Gentlemen who were for the Bill, that tho' both the Language and Writing of the Law should be alter'd, there would be no Danger of losing the use of our ancient Records ; because, as long as we have any such, there will always be some Men, who, either out of Curiosity or for the Sake of Gain, will make it their Business to learn to understand both the Language and Character in which they are wrote . . . : that a very few of such Law Antiquarians will suffise, considering the little Occasion we have in any Law Proceedings to have recourse to any very ancient Records ; and that when they are made use of, they often do more harm than good.[2]

The reformers were successful ; the Bill became law ; [3] and in 1733 Latin lost its last important employment in English records. Henceforward its status in the few and rather obscure connexions in which, for varying periods, it lingered on was to be that of a harmlessly picturesque survival.

2

Medieval Latin

Langlois was critical of those who, never having studied medieval French and Latin, ' think they know them because they understand classical Latin and modern French '.[4] He might more justly have warned those who, never having reached a reasonable proficiency in the classical language, expect not to be handicapped in their dealings with medieval and later Latin. The fact is that the sounder his knowledge of classical Latin the more rapidly and completely will the student master the peculiarities of medieval usage, of which only a few of the more striking can be briefly mentioned here.[5]

Some of the most immediately obvious departures from classical practice are in spelling. At the Norman Conquest, and for nearly a century after, the diphthong *ae* (*oe*)

---

[1] Sir C. H. Firth and Sir R. S. Rait (edd.) : *Acts and Ordinances of the Interregnum* (1911), II, pp. 455–6.

[2] *Political State of Great Britain*, XLII (July–December 1731), p. 181.

[3] 4 Geo. II, c. 26.   [4] *Op. cit.*, p. 29.

[5] For the vocabulary of medieval Latin, see the Bibliography, p. 121 below.

of classical Latin was being written as *e* with a kind of cedilla (the 'tagged' *e*[1]). From about 1150 the tag is absent, and henceforward diphthong *ae* (*oe*) is merged indistinguishably with *e*. Classical *reginae, praesens, caelum* (*coelum*), *coepi* thus become *regine, presens, celum, cepi*.[2] Early in the 13th century *t* standing before *i* and an immediately succeeding vowel (palatalised *t*) begins to be replaced by *c*. The practice becomes general by about 1235, when words such as *gratia, patiens, petii, ratio, tertius* are spelt *gracia, paciens, pecii, racio, tercius*. The rule was never applied when the *t* was preceded by *s*: words like *questio* and *celestium* retained the *t* spelling and did not become *quescio, celescium*. Many 13th-century scribes do not apply the rule when the *t* is preceded by *c*, but write, for example, *exactio, strictius*, often with a ligature between the *c* and the *t*: *exactio, strictius*. But by the end of the 13th century the predominant spelling of such words is with double-*c*: *exaccio, striccius*. The representation of diphthong *ae* by *e* and the substitution, in the situation described, of *c* for *t* remain characteristic of the Latin of English archives for as long as the language is used.

Other features of medieval orthography (some of them persisting into the later period) are the spelling of such words as *damnum, autumnus, calumnia*, with an inserted *p*, to give *dampnum, autumpnus, calumpnia*; the sharpening of compounded *ob-* to *op-* before following *t*, as in *optineo, optulit*; the gutturalising of the *h* in *mihi* and *nihil* to make normal the spellings *michi* and *nichil*; a sporadic preference for *y* over *i* in the initial position, as in *ymago, ymmo, Ydus*; and a strong tendency for *c* in the 'soft' position (before *e* and *i*) to be assimilated to *s*, causing *consilium* to absorb *concilium* completely and giving rise from time to time to spellings such as *sepa* (= *cepa*), *secus* (= *cecus* = classical *caecus*), *nessio* (= *nescio*), *signus* (= *cygnus*), and *sceleriter* and *scelerarius* for *celeriter* and *cellerarius*. Uncertainty, even caprice, about the use of initial *h* is not surprising in a period which had judicial authority for the opinion that '*h* is not a letter' (Hengham, Chief Justice of the Common Pleas, 1304) and that '*abilem* and *habilem* are equally acceptable spellings' (Babington, Chief Justice of the Common Pleas, 1430).[3] Hence *actenus* and *honerare* side by side with *habundancia* and *ympnus*; while Martinmas is regularly *festum sancti Martini in yeme*.

The syntax of medieval Latin, powerfully influenced as it was by the idioms of the Vulgate and of the Romance vernaculars, appears to a modern eye much simpler than that of the classical language. Much of this simplicity is due to the ubiquity of constructions using the conjunction *quod*. In indirect statement the accusative and infinitive of classical usage is almost entirely abandoned for *quod* (sometimes *quia*) with the indicative; *ut*, retained in final clauses, is replaced by *quod* in consecutive ones; and conjunctions formed on *quod* are common. They include *eo quod*, 'because'; *proviso quod*, 'provided that'; *per sic quod*, 'on condition that'; *absque hoc quod*, 'without this, that' (a formula introducing a parenthetical denial); and *eo quod . . . non obstante*, 'notwithstanding that'. Conspicuous carelessness in the handling of the subjunctive is offset in record Latin by an almost pedantic insistence on the future perfect in such phrases as *omnibus ad quos*

---

[1] Illustrated in Plates I (b), II (a) and III (a) below. As the first letter of *ecclesia* the tagged *e* preserves the memory of a common pre-Conquest misspelling *aecclesia*.

[2] When *ae* occurs medievally (as in *escaetor, maeremium, Michael*), it can be taken to be a dissyllable.

[3] See W. C. Bolland: *Manual of Year Book Studies* (Cambridge, 1925), p. 105 and the references there given.

presentes littere pervenerint ; donec aliud preceperimus ; si quis versus eum inde loqui voluerit ; ubicumque tunc fuerimus in Anglia. Prepositions, especially *de, ad,* and *per,* are much more freely used than in classical Latin, and almost always in the senses borne by their French derivatives. In parenthetical clauses the ablative of the gerund often has a force scarcely to be distinguished from that of a present participle : *Willelmus, non cognoscendo terram esse tanti valoris, dicit,* etc.

3

Anglo-Norman French

At its most disciplined and formal (as used, for example, in warrants, deeds, petitions, and Parliamentary proceedings) Anglo-Norman French is fairly obviously deputising for Latin and often preserves in literal translation the expressions, and even the word-order, of recognisable Latin archetypes. Where the influence of Latin models is absent (as in informal correspondence and in the Year Books), written Anglo-Norman wears for a time the appearance of a genuine vernacular—Chaucer's ' Frensh . . . after the scole of Stratford atte Bowe '—with resources of its own. By the end of the 14th century, however, the style of the Year Books suggests that though they were inevitably dealing in French-language clichés and technicalities, the reporters were thinking in English. As early as the reign of Henry IV the English began to intrude into their writing ;[1] and intrusions of this kind became steadily more frequent. The part ultimately played by English in the distinctive language of the law is well illustrated in the famous passage describing how in 1631 a prisoner *ject un Brickbat a le dit Justice que narrowly mist, & pur ceo immediately fuit Indictment drawn per Noy envers le prisoner, & son dexter manus ampute & fix al Gibbet sur que luy mesme immediatement hange in presence de Court.*[2]

A selection of published works which discuss the peculiarities of Anglo-Norman is listed in the Bibliography at p. 121 below ; but the student of archives would be well advised not to spend much time on matters like the phonology and morphology of the language. If he has a working knowledge of modern French and is prepared for frequent and capricious irregularities of usage, the actual archaisms of Anglo-Norman will soon cease to puzzle him. It is unfortunate that the only dictionary that expressly sets out to interpret the language of archives is still Kelham's 18th-century work, which is in no sense scientific and contains a number of ghost-words resulting from mere misreading of manuscript texts. A *Glossary of Law-French,* however, is among the volumes in active preparation for the Selden Society, which already has the distinction of having published Maitland's uniquely valuable essay on the language written in the Year Books of the beginning of the 14th century.

---

[1] Cf. *pendue et let downe arere* and *car perhaps il poet estre qe* cited by W. C. Bolland (op. cit., p. 108) from 1399 and 1402.

[2] Dyer : *Reports* (1688), 188b.

4

The First Steps

Confronted for the first time with an ancient manuscript, the student may be tempted to think that he ought to have begun by learning a series of alphabets. It is, of course, important that he should become familiar with the forms assumed from time to time by the written characters ; but to memorise whole alphabets in a vacuum is not the easiest way to acquire this familiarity, nor does it perceptibly reduce the difficulties of the beginner in reading an actual manuscript. The passage reproduced in Plate XXXII below from a 19th-century memorial tablet in York Minster is hard to read, not because the characters used in it are individually unfamiliar but because the reader's experience has not prepared him for their employment in association. The effect of inscribing the whole passage in letters which are normally met singly, as initial capitals, is one of distortion ; it disturbs the practised reader's unconscious habit of seeking to identify not letters but whole words, or even groups of words, at a single glance.

It is a comparable ' distortion ', often exaggerated by the effects of an unfamiliar system of abbreviation, which causes so many well-written ancient manuscripts to appear illegible to the beginner. If, however, he is prepared to drop the habit of years and to tackle the manuscript letter by letter, he will usually find that very few of the characters in it are genuinely unrecognisable or unidentifiable from the context, and that with practice on manuscripts of the same type or period the number of such characters will tend to shrink very quickly. The letter-forms thus become familiar to him at the same time as he is learning to synthesise them, with growing rapidity, into words. Patiently continued practice is, indeed, the one indispensable means to facility and confidence. The reading of manuscripts is not so much the application of theoretical knowledge as the exercise of a skill, analogous to swimming or bicycle-riding, in the acquisition of which the decisive effort is made by the learner himself.

His first attempts should be on material of which a trustworthy transcript is available —best of all on original manuscripts whose text has been published *verbatim*. For the beginner without access to such originals there is great virtue in well-reproduced facsimiles, accompanied by printed transcripts, like those to be found in the works listed in the Bibliography.[1] The use made of the transcript will vary with the individual. Some students treat it as a check on their own unaided efforts ; others find it more profitable not to attempt to read the manuscript or facsimile until they have first glanced through the opening lines of the transcript.

The material chosen for practice should include a high proportion of formal documents, in order that the student may familiarise himself with the vocabulary and the turns of phrase which he will meet over and over again in his reading of English archives. A close acquaintance with recurrent formulae is well worth cultivating by the transcriber, and not only because it will often enable him to establish with confidence the formal parts of the text of fragmentary or faded manuscripts. In documents written in ' difficult ' or unfamiliar hands any passage that can be read with certainty can be made to provide a key for the reading of the remainder. Starting from the letters, words, or phrases of which he is

[1] See pp. 121–2 below.

sure, the reader can test the plausibility of his conjectures about the others by a process of comparison, after the manner of a man breaking a cipher.

Readings which conflict with sense or grammar should always raise doubts of their accuracy. Not all scribes are in fact faultless, but the wise student will not impute error to the writer until he has excluded the possibility that he may himself be at fault. An attempt has been made in the Table of Confusibilia (p. 120) to suggest some of the resemblances between letters which commonly cause confusion. Where such confusion is possible the student should be guided in his choice of a reading by the sense required in the context, not by the superficial form of the critical letter considered in isolation. It is reasonable, as well as charitable, to assume that a 13th-century ecclesiastic is providing in his will for his aunt (*amita*) rather than for his lady-friend (*amica*), no matter how like a *c* the penultimate letter may look. The risk of misreading is perhaps at its greatest when the manuscript presents a succession of 'minims', the short perpendicular strokes which in varying numbers compose the manuscript letters *i* (often equivalent to *j*[1]), *m*, *n*, and *u* (often equivalent to *v*[1]). Words whose written forms consist wholly or predominantly of successive minims are particularly frequent in Latin: common examples are *nimium*, *minimum, annuum, immunis, innumeri*. Medieval scribes are seldom at pains to indicate the position, or even the presence, of *i*, and after 1200 almost never make any visible distinction between *n* and *u*, *m* and *ni* (*in, ui, iu*), and so forth. The result is that in most medieval writing and in many later hands of a formal nature there is no difference in appearance between, say, *sine* and *sive* ; *munerare* and *numerare* ; *imitare* and *mutare* ; *minor* and *junior* ; *immunis, nummus* and *minimus*. The reader who is faced by a row of minims can but count them carefully and then experiment with their grouping until he succeeds in arranging them in a sequence of letters which will satisfy the sense required. In vernacular documents there is perhaps less danger that a multiplicity of minims will confound the sense,[2] though they often induce incorrect renderings of obsolete spellings. Most beginners have to be warned that the orthodox archaic spellings are *Fraunce, commaund, graunt, verrount, orrount*, etc., not *Frannce, commannd*, etc.

[1] See below, p. 39.
[2] But Newbolt's ' New June ' conceals a somewhat more prosaic ' New Inne '.

CHAPTER III

ABBREVIATION

1

The Medieval System

It was mentioned above that the Act of 1731, besides specifying the language and the style of handwriting to be used in the records it dealt with, provided that those records were to be written ' in words at length and not abbreviated '. The system of abbreviation against which this provision was directed (and which was in consequence now brought formally to an end) had had a very long history.[1] By the date of the Norman Conquest of England the conventions which characterise medieval practice were already firmly established wherever Latin was written. English documents of the 12th century display the system in the most elaborate form it reached in this country: after about 1200 no new abbreviations were introduced into the writing of Latin, and during the later Middle Ages some of those that had formerly been in regular use were gradually discarded.

The medieval system of abbreviation saved time and space by allowing the scribe to drop letters from his writing of individual words. A word of which the beginning is written and the end omitted is said to be suspended: the most extreme form of suspension is, of course, the representation of a whole word by its initial letter alone. When the writer omits a letter or letters from the middle of a word, so that its beginning and end remain, the word is said to be contracted. Except in the circumstances specially noticed below, suspended and contracted words are always found in company with one or another of the variously shaped marks, strokes, or signs, for which our ancestors' generic name was ' tittles ' (Latin *titulus*; Spanish *tilde*). These marks are of two kinds, differentiated according to their functions. ' General ' marks of abbreviation serve simply to warn the reader that he is dealing with an abbreviated form and so to save him from confusing, say, *sic* with the usual suspension of *sicut*, or *do* with the contracted form of *deo*. ' Special,' or significant, marks have the further function of suggesting to the reader the actual letter or letters he must supply in order to expand the abbreviation. It is natural for the beginner in manuscript studies to try to attach fixed meanings to these special marks—to treat each of them, in fact, as if it were a shorthand symbol consistently replacing the same, or approximately the same, letter or syllable; and it might perhaps be convenient for the reader if the function and significance of a mark of abbreviation were always and immediately apparent from its shape. But the medieval system did not aspire to the mechanical precision of a shorthand in which each symbol is given a constant equivalence; and the shape of a mark is not always a certain indication of its function in its context. In particular it will be found that many of the marks which are special or significant when they occur in contractions may be nothing of the kind when they terminate suspended forms.

[1] For its origins and early development and the importance in this connexion of the *Nomina Sacra*, see the works listed in the Bibliography at pp. 121–2 below.

2

Methods of Abbreviation

The following is a short survey of the signs of abbreviation most frequently met in English documents employing Latin.

Sign No. 1. The mark which is most often used to indicate suspension or contraction, without attempting to suggest the specific letter or letters omitted, is made above the abbreviated word. Over a period covering many generations of scribes it is very variously shaped, the extreme of its elaboration being the 'papal knot', illustrated below in the

nobis	inde	autem	de scaccario predicti comitis	sicut	comes Andegavie

nostri	habuerant	racionabili	esse	dei	domini	litteris

ecclesie	graciam	misericordiam	sancte	episcopus

Sign No. 1

abbreviations of *Andegavie* and *episcopus*, which was imported into English use about 1180 and enjoyed some vogue for the next thirty years or so. The predominant form, however, is a horizontal or near-horizontal dash set over short letters and passing through the ascenders of tall ones. In early documents this sign, whatever form it takes, is a separate stroke of the pen, made with some deliberation, but from the 13th century it is increasingly often found, especially in suspensions, as a mere extension upward and backward of the letter last written before it.

Sign No. 2. This is not, in the overwhelming majority of English documents, a discernibly different sign from No. 1, but a distinctive or special use of it. Placed above

immo	in regno	fratrum	totam	sapientium	immunis

anime	homines	omnino	omnium parentum	nominaverit	libertatem

Sign No. 2

vowels it indicates the omission of one or more nasal consonants (*m, n*).   By reducing the number of minims in the line of writing it may thus be an aid to reading.   In *heres, clericus*, the adjective *liber*, and their derivatives, and in a few other words, this sign is drawn through the ascenders of *h, l*, and *b* to represent suppressed *er*.

Sign No. 3.   A general mark of abbreviation frequent in 12th-century documents consists of a vertical wavy line, somewhat like a crude narrow S.   In the second half of the century this mark was increasingly often chosen to replace *er* and *re* (a function previously discharged by a short horizontal stroke or one resembling a short-stemmed Arabic 7).   By the 13th century it had assumed the shape, which it long retained, of a backward

terre	eternam	monasterio	fuerint	vertere	fraternitatis
veritatis	preterea	presentes littere	gracia	juratores dicunt quod	

Sign No. 3

curve terminating in a bold pendent comma, and was so regularly used in contractions suppressing *er* and *re* that it is often described as the ' *er (re)* abbreviation '.   In so far as no other superior sign (except No. 2 in the few instances above mentioned) specifically replaces these letters, the description is justified.   Exceptionally this sign can have the value of *ir (ri)* ; and in one word—*uxor*—it is regularly written for *or*.   But it never ceased to be usable as an entirely general mark of abbreviation ; and especially in suspensions it will often be found so used.   In later documents, when its size and definiteness have been reduced and it may be only an inconspicuous addition to the letter to which it is linked, its presence is sometimes easy to overlook.

Sign No. 4.   A superior mark which may often be likened to a small single-bowled *a* with a curving tail-like appendage (but which admits of substantial variation from this

teneamur	audituris	teneretur	servituris	continetur

Sign No. 4

form) is to be read as equivalent to *ur* or, on very rare occasions, *ru*.   It is used in both suspension and contraction.

Sign No. 5.   Final *us* is consistently indicated by a superior sign which, within fairly wide limits, may be said to resemble an Arabic 9.   This sign is not really common as a mark of contraction except in formations like *ejusdem* and *cujusdam*, but when it does occur medially its value may be either *us* or *os*.   Its use in abbreviating *post* and compounds containing *post* is noticed below.

tempus melius plenius ipsius ejus tenuimus

potius opus illius nichilominus hujus hujusmodi

Sign No. 5

Sign No. 6. In outline this mark (standing for *con-* or *com-*) often resembles No. 5, but differs from it in always appearing in the line of writing, in which it is normally ranged with the descending letters. For the reader there is sometimes a risk of confusion between it and the letter *q*.

controversie inconvulsum confirmaverunt confirmavi confectis

Sign No. 6

Sign No. 7. This sign, which in early post-Conquest documents retains its original appearance, that of a modern semicolon, soon developed a cursive form reminiscent of an Arabic 3. In some 14th-century and later hands there is no observable difference between it and the letter *z*. It is always a mark of suspension placed in the line of writing, and in English practice is almost confined to the truncation of two classes of words : the first, datives and ablatives in *-bus*, in which it replaces the final *us* ; the second, words ending in

omnibus fidelibus precibus heredibus

absque itaque cuicumque quoque de omnibus rebus usque ad

Sign No. 7

the enclitic or suffix *-que*, in which it replaces the final *ue*. In some few words its function is general : the commonest are compounds of *libet* and *licet* (*viz.*, as an abbreviation of *videlicet*, has survived to our own times), but *s3*, *p3*, *d3*, representing *set* (= *sed*), *patet*, *debet*, are all found, the first of them being especially frequent.

Sign No. 8. Words suspended at a letter whose concluding stroke, on or near the base-line, is approximately horizontal commonly carry, as a sign that they are suspended, an obliquely curving mark through this final stroke.   The letter *k*, in some of its forms, and the capital *R* particularly lent themselves to this treatment, of which the medical prescriber's ℞ (a suspension of *Recipe*) is a surviving example.   The letter, however, which in practice most often carried this mark of suspension was the so-called 'Arabic-2' small *r*, which was the form of *r* consistently written after the round-bodied letters *a* and *o*.   Genitive

| animarum | litigiorum | clericorum | bonorum | suorum |

Sign No. 8

plurals of the first and second declensions, employing this *r* and suspended at the earliest point at which the grammatical case had been made apparent, provide by far the commonest occasions for the use of this sign—so much the commonest that the Arabic-2 *r* carrying it came quite early to be regarded as a 'significant symbol' for *-rum*, and the truncated forms of *Saresberia* and *Blandford Forinseca*, for example, were wrongly extended to *Sarum* and *Blandford Forum*.

Sign No. 9.   A looped vertical mark of suspension frequent from the 14th century onwards has a purely general function in Latin-language documents.   The letters to which

| tenendum | quod | belles (Eng.) | paces (Eng.) |

Sign No. 9

it is most often attached are *d*, *f*, and *g*.   Though it is in origin and by position a sign of suspension, its use in the common late abbreviation of *quod* is really to mark a contraction. Its value in English-language writing is mentioned below (p. 37).

The marks associated with the letters *p* and *q* are worthy of special attention.   The words *pro*, *per*, *pre*, and *post*, and compounds containing them, are by most writers so carefully distinguished in abbreviation that in any one document the reader has seldom any excuse for confusing their appearance.   He should note that in company with *p* Sign No. 3 stands invariably for *re*, and never for *er*.   Sign No. 5 is used with *p* to provide an abbreviation for *post*, commoner in early documents than late ones.   The *per* abbreviation also does duty, notably in *pars* and its numerous derivatives, for *par*, and in the oblique cases of *tempus* and *corpus* for *por*.   Beginners often have difficulty with the group of abbreviations involving the letter *q*, and are particularly apt to render the compendia for *quando* (*qñ*) and *quoniam* erroneously as *quin* and *quum*.   This last is in fact a spelling unknown to the medieval Latinist, who always writes *cum* for preposition and conjunction alike.

The abbreviation $\overline{Jhs}$ $\overline{Xps}$, or $\overline{Jhc}$ $\overline{Xpc}$, for the name of Jesus Christ arises from the practice of reproducing in Latin texts the contracted form of the Greek ιΗϹΟΥϹ ΧΡΙϹΤΟϹ. *Xp* is also used for Chr(ist-) in the abbreviation of the derivatives *Christianus*, *Christopherus*,

etc. ; and in early post-Conquest documents contractions of *spiritus* and *episcopus* sometimes feature a final *c* which has the value of a Greek sigma.

Words reduced by abbreviation to a single letter are sometimes called *sigla*. Some
of them bear no abbreviative tittle but are preceded and followed by a full point. The
commonest words so treated in English documents (apart from Christian names represented

pro	professionis	promittent	prout	propter
perpetue	recuperare	persone	partem	parysshe	corpore	persona
predictum	presideat	presentes	presumat	postquam	postmodum
quod	quam	quia	quoniam	quare

only by their initial letters) are *scilicet* (.s.), *id est* (.i.), and *enim* (.n.). *Hoc* is rendered
by *h* surmounted by a dot (ḣ), to be distinguished from *h* traversed by Sign No. 1, which
stands for *hec*. The single letter *l* traversed by the same sign replaces *vel*.

Contraction is often indicated by the use of superscript letters. These letters may,
in a fashion still current, simply represent the termination or an important constituent
of the contracted word, as in m^i (= *michi*), t^i (= *tibi*), v^o (= *vero*), m^o (= *modo*), u^i (= *ubi*),

ampersands		eciam	etc.
quilibet quolibet	scilicet	est	process marks

Abbreviation by symbols

and in the more surprising g^a, g^i, g^o, which stand respectively for *erga*, *igitur*, and *ergo*.
But vowels (much the commonest are *a* and *i*) may also be written above abbreviated words
to suggest the suppression of the letter *r* before, or, very rarely, after, the superscript vowel.
Thus $t^a ns$ = *trans*, $p^i or$ = *prior*, $c^u cem$ = *crucem*, $icc^i co$ = *iccirco*. Any of the vowels
except *u* may be placed above *q* and in this position argues the omission of preceding *u*.
Thus $q^a m$ = *quam*, $q^i ppe$ = *quippe*, q^o = *quo*. It is worth remarking that by most scribes

H.E.D.—C

superscript *a* is given a distinctive form which is often much more like that of *u* than of any *a* appearing in the line of writing.

The symbols substituted in English archives for whole words are only two. The ampersand, which over the years takes a variety of forms, does duty in Latin documents of all periods for the complete word *et*, and in some early ones for the syllable *et* occurring in other words. Surmounted by Sign No. 1 it represents *eciam* (= *etiam*). Most English scribes observe a rule that when it is the first word in a sentence *Et* must be written out and not replaced by the ampersand. A symbol more or less closely resembling the mathematical sign for division ($\div$) represents *est* in documents of the 12th and early 13th centuries, later losing this function but retaining another, which is to serve in the margins of plea rolls as a process mark or indication that a writ or summons has issued.

3

' Record Type '

Towards the end of the 18th century the demand of antiquarians for accurate texts led to the cutting of special ' record types '—roman founts which included the means of representing in print the signs, devices and conventions of abbreviated medieval manuscript. Between 1783, when the text of Domesday Book was printed in the first and most elaborate of the record types, and 1900, when the Pipe Roll Society issued the last of its volumes to employ the medium, a large number of English manuscript records were published in editions which purported to transcribe the originals *literatim* and to preserve all their abbreviations. The manuscript and the record-type version of a passage in a 14th-century document are reproduced in juxtaposition in Plate VII. Since 1900 times have changed. ' The considerations which led to the use of " record type " for published records now appear to have lost their validity, and what is really required by most people is, not a hybrid facsimile in special type or even in ordinary type adorned with a clumsy apparatus of palaeographic notanda, but " a version modernised to meet the exigencies of the existing system of typography [and reproducing] the original manuscript extended according to the indications afforded by the scribe." ' [1]

Record type was devised, and has usually been discussed, purely as a means of transmitting texts ; but record-type editions, studied in conjunction with the manuscripts (or photographic copies of the manuscripts) from which they are taken, can be very helpful to the beginner wishing to familiarise himself with the system of abbreviation described above. He will find that the editor is very apt to rationalise the scribe's use of the signs of abbreviation : that whereas the manuscript makes no distinction of shape between Sign No. 1 and Sign No. 2, the printed text will represent the first by a curved *tilde* and the second by a flat horizontal bar ; that Sign No. 3 is printed only when the scribe has used it with the value of *er*, *re*, etc., being replaced by Sign No. 1 on the occasions when it occurs in the manuscript as a purely general mark ; and that Sign No. 1 is normally also substituted

[1] *Notes for the Guidance of Editors of Record Publications* (British Records Association, 1946), p. 8, quoting Hubert Hall : *Studies in English Official Historical Documents* (Cambridge, 1908), p. 394.

by the editor for the scribe's Sign No. 9. These departures from the usage of the manuscript may seem to weaken editorial claims to have furnished an absolutely faithful reproduction, but for the apprentice reader they help to make the record-type text a half-way stage towards the interpretation of the abbreviations.

4

The Treatment of Proper Names

Students setting out to make extended transcripts of documents written in Latin are sometimes uncertain how they should render abbreviated proper names. Where the name abbreviated is known to be the consistently spelt Latin equivalent of an English one, there is no difficulty of principle in treating it, for the purposes of extended transcription, in exactly the same way as any other abbreviated Latin word in the same document. The names of which the abbreviated forms may be extended with confidence can be grouped as follows.

(a) *Christian Names.* Nearly all the Christian names in common English use between the Norman Conquest and the 18th century had Latin equivalents whose spelling scarcely varied throughout the period (the medieval *Willelmus*, for example, holds its ground, even in late documents, against the post-Renaissance *Gulielmus*) and whose contraction and suspension follows conventions settled at a very early date (such, for example, as that which recognised *Ed'us* as the compendium for *Edmundus*, while *Edwardus* was shortened to *Ed'r'us*). There is seldom room for doubt about the full form of any of these names represented by an abbreviation.

(b) *Surnames.* In early medieval documents surnames describing the trades, nationalities, parentage, and physical or other attributes of their bearers are commonly translated into Latin; for example, *Johannes Pistor, Philippus Carpentarius, Nicholaus Anglicus, Jordanus Brito, Adam filius Hugonis, Matillis filia Ranulfi, Henricus Albus, Walterus Parvus.* On the occasions when they are abbreviated such names offer no difficulty to the transcriber.

(c) *Place-names.* Vernacular place-names of self-evident meaning are also often translated in Latin documents, and forms like *Novum Castrum* (Newcastle), *Bellum* (Battle), *Pons Altus* (Highbridge), and *Album Monasterium* (Whitchurch) are persistent. Apart from such translations there are available recognised Latin or sham-Latin names for a number of well-known English places, such as *Eboracum* for York, *Westmonasterium* for Westminster, *Beverlacum* for Beverley, *Cantuaria* for Canterbury, and *Oxonia* for Oxford. Comparable with these names, and for the most part as readily extended when they occur in abbreviation, are the Latin adjectives in *-ensis*, formed from place-names, which distinguish bishops, dioceses, and various other ecclesiastical dignitaries and institutions; for example, *episcopus Wigorniensis, diocesis Eliensis, ecclesia cathedralis Exoniensis.*

But some abbreviated place-names, even though they appear to be Latin, cannot safely be extended in transcript. *Oxon', Ebor',* and *Wigorn',* for example, were early made to serve as abbreviations of the names of counties, peerage titles, etc., by scribes who were little concerned with what, in their new use, their suppressed terminations might be supposed to be. The reader who is satisfied that *Sar'*, in an ecclesiastical context, abbreviates an adjective in *-ensis* at all may well hesitate to decide which of twelve possible alternatives is the full spelling implied at any given date.[1]

Non-latinised surnames are preponderantly made up at all times of those which derive from the bearers' places of origin or abode and may therefore be regarded as place-names for the present purpose. The remainder comprise untranslated surnames in English or French describing their bearers' trades, nationalities, parentage, or personal characteristics. Such names are seldom abbreviated, but they do occasionally end in a mark of suspension, which is best rendered in transcription by an apostrophe.

By far the greatest number of place-names occurring in English archives will be in an unmistakably English form. Up to about the end of the 12th century there are fitful attempts at latinising some of them : names ending in English *-ton* (*-tun*), for example, are turned into more or less plausible-looking first-declension Latin nouns by the addition of the appropriate Latin termination, which is either written out or sufficiently indicated. There were obvious limits to the possibilities of such *ad hoc* latinisation, and scribes must soon have begun to wonder whether they need venture overtly upon it. The ' Latin ' suffix was accordingly replaced in their writing by a mark of suspension, which, even if it began as a conscious compromise, rapidly became and for centuries remained the conventional accompaniment of almost all vernacular place-names[2] in Latin documents. The transcriber need not seek any ' value ' for this mark, which should appear in his extended version as an apostrophe. The same is true of those cases in which there is suspension of more than the hypothetical original Latin termination, as in *Berk'*, *Warr'*.

5

Abbreviation in Anglo-Norman

The medieval system of abbreviation was evolved for use with Latin, and the writers of Anglo-Norman French could never have been more than partially successful in applying it to their own purposes. In practice, Anglo-Norman documents are very much less heavily abbreviated than the Latin ones contemporary with them. There was obvious convenience in taking from Latin the four *p*-abbreviations, which provided compendia for French *par* (on occasion *per-*), *pre-*, *pro-*, and *puis* ; and the addition of Sign No. 4 to *p* gave a frequently used abbreviation for *pur* (= *pour*). Contraction was restricted to a relatively small number of common words : in some cases, for example *n're*, *l're*, *b'n* (for *nostre*, *lettre*, *bien*), it had actual Latin precedents ; in others, for example *ch'r* (for *chivaler*) or *ch're* (for *chartre*), it was a new application of the principle. In the Year Books (but perhaps nowhere else) Sign No. 5 is freely used as a general mark of suspension. Spellings like *qiconqe*, *evesqe*, etc., are so common in Anglo-Norman French that abbreviations

---

[1] Possible variations on a basic *Saresberiensis* are the doubling of the first *r*, the substitution of *i* for *e* following it, and the substitution of *i* or *u* for the *e* following the *b*.

[2] The chief exceptions are names ending in *-e*, *-by*, and *-ham*. For the last of these it was long the fashion to write *-h^{a}m*, though no abbreviation can be intended.

involving the letter *q* often pose the question whether or not in the extended transcript *u* should be supplied after *q*. The practice of the scribe, so far as it can be observed elsewhere in the document, does not always give unambiguous guidance.

6

Abbreviation in English-language Documents

English was even less fitted than Anglo-Norman French to make full use of the devices intended to shorten the labour of writing Latin. The earliest application of the medieval system to English was, as has been seen above, in the writing, in Latin documents, of native proper names, which were terminated by a mark of suspension to preserve the fiction that they were declinable Latin words. When archives came to be written in the English language there was thus already established a tradition associating the general marks of suspension with a large number of characteristically English word-endings; and it is presumably to this fact that we owe the freedom with which in the 15th and early 16th centuries documents in English are peppered with marks which seem to serve no abbreviative purpose whatever. If in their original employment, such marks had ever implied the suppression of Latin case-endings to English words, it is certain that no such case-endings were implicit in a document written entirely in English; and it would probably not be far wrong to describe as otiose any mark in such a document which does not obviously replace letters necessary to the sense.

When, in the first third or so of the 16th century, English scribes had rid themselves of the habit of treating certain typical word-endings as ' suspended ' forms, the traces of the old system surviving in documents written in English began to decrease. Later English documents will rarely be found to exhibit more of them than the three *p*-compendia, for *per-* (*par-*), *pro-*, and *pre-*, which were useful in abbreviating Romance derivatives; Sign No. 9, which is used finally with the value *-es*, *-is*, *-ys*, or even plain *-s*, according to the writer's taste in forming the plural; the conventional contractions *l're* and *m're*, adopted from French to abbreviate *letter* and *matter*; and such vestigial contraction of words in *-ation*, *-ition*, etc. (still spelt with medieval Latin *c*), as *-ac'on*, *-ic'on*, etc. A few abbreviations were coined for use in English-language writing; a feature of them is the use of superior letters in contractions: w^t, w^{ch}, M^r, Matie, for *with*, *which*, *Master*, *Majestie*. (The point at which M^r, as a title, begins to be ' Mister ' and consequently incapable of extension seems to lie somewhere in the reign of Elizabeth I.) In y^t and y^e, the *y* is a survival in a corrupt form of the obsolete letter *thorn*, which had the sound of *th*. The form y^e is sometimes condemned as erroneous on the ground that the superior *e* implies abbreviation where there has been none.

7

Abbreviation in the Later Period

In the meantime, Latin documents were themselves much less resourcefully abbreviated than their medieval forerunners had been. It has already been suggested that where Latin is used in this later period it reflects the survival not only of medieval institutions but of medieval practice and phraseology. There is thus a tendency to rely on the familiar word-order of common form to justify the use of a system of abbreviation which comparatively seldom departs from simple suspension eked out by a few compendia. This tendency is increased by the ease with which writers uncertain of their Latin grammar could conceal their ignorance of the correct terminations simply by omitting them. The procedure could not be more frankly expounded than in the advice given to his clerk, Dulman, by Ignoramus the lawyer in Ruggle's play of 1615 : ' Si non potes scribere verum Latinum, sicut ego scribo, abbrevia verba per demidium [*sic*] ; scribe cum dasho, ut multi faciunt ; sic nec facies errorem in Latino nec errorem in Lege.' [1]

[1] G. Ruggle : *Ignoramus* (ed. J. S. Hawkins, 1787), IV. viii.

CHAPTER IV

SCRIBAL CONVENTIONS AND EXPEDIENTS

1

The Characters

For writing their own language the Saxons used the Latin alphabet, to which they added a few characters to express certain distinctively English sounds. Two of these characters, *wen* and *thorn*, may occasionally be met in post-Conquest documents in Latin. *Wen* (ƿ), which renders the sound of *w*, is very rare indeed: at the date of the Norman Conquest it was in process of supersession by *w* itself, which was firmly established in England by the beginning of the 11th century and is written throughout Domesday Book. *Thorn* (þ), on the other hand, though never really common, continued for about a hundred and fifty years after the Conquest to be used sporadically in archives as a means of representing the sound of *th*. When, in the 15th century, documents began to be written extensively in English, *thorn* returned again to archive contexts as a convenient equivalent for *th*, especially in the initial position. During the 16th century it was gradually assimilated in form to *y* and provided later writers with an intermittently used method of abbreviating *the* and *that*.[1] The Middle-English letter *yogh* (ȝ), used for certain values of *g* and *y*, is not uncommon in vernacular words in documents of the 14th and 15th centuries, in which it is increasingly confused in form with *z*.

The convention which treats the forms *i* and *u* as vowels and the forms *j* and *v* as consonants did not gain general acceptance in England until the beginning of the 18th century. For earlier writers *i* and *j* on the one hand and *u* and *v* on the other were variant forms of one letter; and *Judas* was a perfectly permissible anagram of *Davis*. In Latin documents of all periods the *i-longa* or *j* form is often chosen for the second of two successive *i*'s, especially in the final position: *hijs, ijdem, alij, Marcij, Georgij*. In medieval and most subsequent practice position also determined the choice between *u* and *v*, the latter being preferred for use initially and the former elsewhere, so that the normal forms are *vt, vua, nouus, vpon, neuer*. But there is no lack of 16th-century and later examples of disregard of this rule, such as *pervse* and (especially in italic hands) *uery*. Some 13th-century scribes, conscious of the composition of *w*, treat it as the equivalent of *vu* and write, for example, *wlnus, wlpes, wlt*, and (in French) *ws*.

[1] See above, p. 37.

2

Numerals

For about five centuries after the Norman Conquest the system of numerals employed in English writing was essentially the Roman one. The few peculiarities which distinguish its use are unlikely to cause the reader much difficulty : they seem, indeed, to have been evolved to remove the risks of confusion and to reduce the ease with which a number, once written, could be altered. For as long as Roman numerals are the normal first choice of the writers of English documents, the letters composing them are in the same cursive forms as they would be in any other context, and there is a very marked preponderance of minuscule (or small-letter) forms. Despite the convention, described above, which ordinarily governed the choice between the *u* and the *v* forms, from about the middle of the 12th century the symbol for *5*, whether in the initial position or elsewhere, is invariably *v*, presumably because of the close resemblance, in a cursive hand, between *u* and *ii*. Final and isolated units are in the *i-longa* or *j* form, which lessens the danger of confusion between, say, *vj* (= 6) and *vi* (the ablative of *vis*), *vij* and French *vn*, *viij* and Latin *vni*. The normal forms are *iiij*, *xiiij*, etc., not *iv*, *xiv*, etc., which are very late. In medieval documents numbers are usually distinguished from words by having a full point before and after them. In 15th-century and later accounts numerals expressing sums of money are regularly preceded by an elaborate lozenge-shaped mark terminating in a dash or flourish. When the dash is short and the mark is thus brought close to the numeral it precedes, care is necessary to ensure that it is not mistaken for the contemporary *c* (which it often superficially resembles) and given a numerical value. The native practice of counting in scores is reflected in the persistent preference for forms like $\overset{xx}{iiij}$ (almost invariable for 80), $\overset{xx}{vij}$ (= 140), $\overset{xx}{ix}$ (= 180), etc., over the traditional Roman-figure expressions. Numbers over 600 are likelier to be in such forms as *vj^c*, *viij^c*, than in combinations with *d* (for 500). On very rare occasions *c* symbolises not the ' short ' hundred of five score but the ' long ' or ' great ' one, of six, so that *cl*, for example, is 170, *ccx* is 250, and *cccxl* is 400. When *c* has the value 120, the symbol for 100 becomes $\overset{xx}{v}$ or *ll*, and 90 has to be expressed by *iiij.x* or *lxxxx* : thus $\overset{xx}{v}.xj$ = 111 ; $c\overset{xx}{v}.ij$ = 222 ; *clxxxxix* = 219 ; *cllxij* = 232 ; *ccllj* = 341. If both the long and the short hundred figure in the same account, some commodities being reckoned in one and some in the other, they may be distinguished as *c^{ma}* and *c^{mi}* (*centum majus* and *centum minus*). Sometimes *c* is followed by a genitive and represents the noun *centena* (French *centaine*) ; and on occasion it means not ' a hundred ' but ' a hundredweight '. Ordinals occurring in English-language documents in the form *xxijth*, etc., are intended to be read as ' two and twentieth ', etc.

The persistence of Roman numerals needs no particular emphasis, since their use, though today increasingly restricted to learned and ceremonious contexts, has not yet died out. They continued to be written in English archives long after Arabic numerals had become commonplace—occasionally, indeed, in the 16th century side by side with them, as in Plate XX (a) below. The choice for writers between Roman and Arabic numerals remained very largely a matter of taste—even of caprice—until Englishmen generally had learned to use Arabic numerals for the purposes of written calculation.

The unsuitability of Roman numerals for these purposes is obvious enough : the absence of a written symbol for zero is alone sufficient to keep arithmetic primitive. The processes of addition and subtraction were accordingly carried out in medieval times on a form of abacus or counting-frame. At the English royal Exchequer the abacus consisted of a checked cloth (*scaccarium*) which actually gave its name to the department. Each vertical column of squares on this cloth represented a different monetary denomination : from right to left, farthings, pence, shillings, pounds, scores of pounds, hundreds of pounds, thousands of pounds, scores of thousands of pounds, and so on. Counters were placed in these vertical columns to express amounts of money ; and the value of each counter was determined not only by the column in which it was placed but also by its position relatively to the base line running horizontally across the columns. Thus in each column units of the denomination are on or below the line (farthings are always below it) ; in all the columns, except those for pence and farthings, five units are expressed by a single counter above the line and on the right, and in the shillings, pounds, and thousands-of-pounds columns ten units are expressed by a single counter above the line and on the left ; and in the pence column a single counter placed centrally above the line stands for 6d. Examples will make this clear :

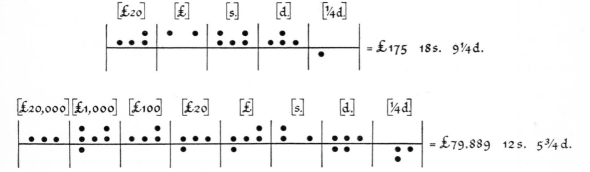

In each column the number of counters placed on the line does not normally exceed three : if it is desired to express a fourth (or, in the pence column, a fifth) unit, the additional counter(s) will be found below the line.

The method of expression described above (which was not confined to the royal Exchequer) is known as the 'auditors' use'. A 'use' or 'form' which employed the same basic principle to express sums of money, but placed the denominations vertically one above another instead of horizontally, was called the 'merchants' use'. The procedure followed in calculation, which is the same in both 'uses', need not be discussed here, where the system of monetary expression is mentioned because the margins of audited accounts, particularly in the 15th and 16th centuries, will often be found to contain groups of manuscript dots which are in effect diagrams of the abacus and reproduce in writing the relative positions of the counters. In such diagrams the horizontal base-line is never actually drawn.

3

Arabic Numerals

Arabic numerals seem to have first come to the notice of European writers towards the end of the 10th century, and as early as 1202 an Italian mathematician, Leonardo of Pisa, published a Latin treatise showing how they could be used to carry out the four elementary operations of arithmetic. In England, however, it was not until the 16th century was well advanced that they began to be generally employed for the purpose of calculation; and even in their capacity of mere graphic alternatives for Roman figures they are not really common in English documents before about 1530. There seems, it is true, to be no English parallel for the kind of express prohibition which elsewhere excluded them from official accounts[1] on the ground that they could be too easily altered; but when the great Lord Burghley died in 1598, after a lifetime spent at the centre of English affairs, he had virtually never used Arabic numerals except to write the year of grace.

Arabic numerals: (*a*) 2–10 (13th cent.); (*b*) 40–49 (14th cent.); (*c*) 92–98, 100 (16th cent.)

Throughout the medieval period the commonest use to which Arabic figures were put in this country was the numbering of the folios or pages of books, the membranes of rolls, and so forth. Numerals serving this purpose can seldom be very closely dated: all that can be said with confidence about most of them is that they are later than the texts with which they are associated. Precisely datable examples of Arabic figures—that is to say examples which are undoubtedly contemporary with the documents containing them—do, however, occur often enough to make discernible the broad lines on which these numerals developed in England from about the middle of the 13th century.[2]

At no time do they present any real difficulties of reading. At their most archaic and unfamiliar they are most likely to be met in the sequences of cataloguing, foliation and pagination which make identification easy; and elsewhere the writer of numbers, who can seldom expect his intention to be inferred from their context, is necessarily at pains to form his figures clearly. The chief risks of error run by the modern reader of early Arabic

---

[1] At Florence between 1299 and 1347, and at Frankfurt in 1494. See G. Battelli: *Lezioni di Paleografia* (3rd edn., Vatican, 1949), p. 219, and the authorities there cited.

[2] Early specimens among the Public Records are to be found in Shropshire Eyre Rolls for 1256 and 1292 (J.I. 1/734 and 739); a Dorset Eyre Roll of 1268 (J.I. 1/202); the accounts, dated 1270–1, of lands belonging to the see of Canterbury (Ministers' Accounts 1128/1); and the endorsements of certain writs of *diem clausit extremum* of 1292–3 (Chancery Inquisitions post mortem, Edw. I, 65/7).

numerals are that he may ' get them out of period ' (misreading, say, the medieval *2* as *7*), and that he may on occasion fail to recognise them as numerals at all (when, for example, early forms are written marginally in isolation).

In early examples *0* is often traversed by a long stroke slightly inclined from the vertical and projecting some distance above and below. This feature continues to be common until the end of the 15th century and does not wholly disappear until the middle of the 16th.

From the beginning *1* is almost always readily recognisable. During the 16th and 17th centuries it frequently begins and ends with a small hook, to the left at the top and to the right at the base, after the manner of the modern printed italic *i*; and in this form it is occasionally read by beginners as *2*, though the contemporary *2* is in fact conspicuously different from it.

At its first appearance in English archives *2* consists of two strokes and somewhat resembles a crude modern *7*, but by the middle of the 14th century this form has been abandoned in favour of a Z-shaped figure which soon develops into the pattern now familiar in print. The horizontal base-stroke is a prominent feature from the time of its first addition: jutting well to the left it serves to distinguish *2* very sharply from the *i*-shaped *1*.

A form of *3* common in the 15th century and the first half of the 16th has the tail turned towards the right, like the contemporary descending *z*, by which it may well have been influenced. This form is occasionally varied by one in which the tail is vertical.

The last of the ten digits to achieve its modern form is *4*. Until late in the 16th century it was composed of two curved lines, crossed near their bases and meeting at their other extremities. Its recumbent appearance and the fact that the enclosed space is not triangular sometimes disguise its identity from the beginner. The uprightness associated with the modern form occurs occasionally before 1500 but is not usual until about the middle of the 16th century.

The predominant medieval form of *5* resembles a splayed and angular letter *h* with its third stroke descending vertically. Variations on this basic form retain a general likeness to *h* until the evolution of a more economically written form consisting of a single stroke which, as it descends, curves gently first to the left and then to the right. The short horizontal stroke at the head, which is nowadays regarded as an integral part of the figure, does not appear until fairly late in the 16th century.

The chief characteristic of early forms of *6* is their comparative squatness. The top-most stroke does not ascend, as it does in the modern form, and is often almost horizontal. The figure thus tends to resemble the capital *G* contemporary with it. A less open form, which is also common, is rather like a Greek sigma.

Until early in the 16th century *7* consistently takes the form of a baseless isosceles triangle or a sanserif capital lambda, but thereafter it quickly develops its modern appearance.

Except for one exotic form, which suggests a recumbent capital *S* and occurs from time to time in documents of the 17th and early 18th centuries, *8* is usually recognisable from the Middle Ages onwards.

The same is true of *9*. Occasionally in the 15th and 16th centuries it bears a strong resemblance to the contemporary small *g*, in conformity with the tendency figures always show to approximate to letters written with a similar action of the pen.

4

Punctuation

It has been said that since the medieval book was meant to be read aloud, its punctuation was ' designed to save the reader's breath, rather than to convey the grammatical construction to the eye '.[1] But these purposes are not mutually exclusive ; indeed, they must be reconciled if the reader is to succeed in transmitting the writer's meaning.   In their observations on punctuation Alcuin of York in the 8th century, Friar Roger Bacon in the 13th, and Guarini of Verona in the 15th, all make this clear.   Alcuin enjoins the proper pointing of sacred texts so ' that the reader in church will not read them incorrectly or perhaps fall abruptly silent in front of his devout brethren '.[2]   Guarini defines a point as ' a sign which either by its shape or by the pause it represents (*vel figura vel mora sua*) separates clauses, marks off units of sense (*distinguit sensus*), refreshes the mind, and leaves an interval for thought '.[3]   The separation of clauses not only clarified the sense and enabled a text to be read aloud with the correct intonation but brought out the calculated rhythms and cadences which were an indispensable feature of elegant prose. That some significance was attached at an early date to the punctuation of business documents is suggested by the attitude of the legal profession.   In 1210 a hopeful canonist challenged the genuineness of a papal bull ' *quia punctus deerat* ',[4] but lawyers in general seem soon to have come to regard the presence of points as a potentially greater embarrassment than their absence.   In England formal documents carry less and less punctuation until the 15th century, when examples of completely unpunctuated instruments begin to be common.

Perhaps the first task for the beginner is to satisfy himself which of the dots in a medieval manuscript are intended to punctuate it and which of them serve other purposes. In the earliest documents with which this book is concerned there are normally only two forms of genuine stop—the full point and the mark which, resembling a modern semicolon inverted and reversed, constituted the medieval comma.   Unfortunately the full point served throughout the Middle Ages a number of other purposes besides punctuation.   We have already seen that it was used to enclose Roman numerals and the *sigla* ; some 13th-century scribes insert a full point after every abbreviated word (as an additional, not an alternative, indication of abbreviation) ; and often the point seems to be no more than evidence of the place at which a scribe rested his pen between writing one passage and memorising the next.   Where it does seem to be intended to punctuate the manuscript its value, in terms of modern punctuation, is often obscure.   In an undated manuscript from Vallombrosa described as ' *vetus* ' in the Appendix to Ruinart's 1709 edition of Mabillon's *De Re Diplomatica*[5] it is called a *colum* and defined as ' a plain point placed at the end of a clause when the whole sense is complete '.   There are few medieval English documents which would support this as an exhaustive account of its functions.

[1] V. H. Galbraith : *The Literacy of the Medieval English Kings* (1935), p. 5.

[2] Carmen, LXVII, 7–10 : *Per cola distinguant proprios et commata sensus,* | *Et punctos ponant ordine quosque suo,* | *Ne vel falsa legat taceat vel forte repente* | *Ante pios fratres lector in ecclesia.* Frobenius [Forster] : *Alcuini Opera* (Ratisbon, 1777), Vol. II, p. 211.   Cf. Roger Bacon, *Opus Tertium*, c. 62, and *Comp. Stud. Phil.*, c. 8.

[3] Quoted, *s.v.* punctare, by Du Cange in the *Glossarium*.

[4] E. Baluze : *Epistolae Innocentii III* (Paris, 1682), Vol. II, p. 434.   [5] p. 638.

Of the medieval comma the Vallombrosa manuscript says that it is used ' at a place where the clause may be complete but some addition is contemplated '. Almost all that can be safely remarked about its use in English archives is that it has a value less than that

Medieval punctuation, distinguishing two types of ablative

of the modern full stop—how much less depends on the taste of the writer and perhaps also of the reader. In manuscript service books it is used, as in printed ones the colon is used today, to ' point ' matter intended to be chanted or sung. Towards the end of the 13th century it begins to develop in business documents a rapidly written cursive form, which by the middle of the following century is being executed in a single stroke of the unlifted pen and henceforward resembles a modern tick with a curved or broken back. But before the end of the 14th century it had passed out of use.

The remaining marks discussed in the Vallombrosa manuscript, though some of them are there credited with functions which they did not discharge in this country, will provide a convenient series of headings for an account of English practice.

The first of these marks, to which the manuscript gives the name *suspensivus*, is our own comma (,), which does not appear in English documents until the 16th century. It seems to have reached this country through the printer, being first found with roman types about 1521 and with black-letter types about fifteen years later.[1] In the meantime it had been adopted by the writers of manuscript and becomes common in archives as the century proceeds. Its predecessor as a means of marking a short pause was the *virgula*, an oblique stroke like the one the printer calls the ' shilling-stroke ', which was freely used for about a hundred years from the middle of the 15th century and might on occasion serve to conclude a completed sentence. From time to time during the 14th century names, particularly place-names, forming a long catalogue in a narrative passage may be marked off from each other by very short vertical strokes on the base-line. Such marks are never used to mark off the clauses in a sentence, and their function in a catalogue of names is to enable the reader to avoid wrong combinations in such a list as, for example, *Sutton Magna Norton Parva Weston Aston Clinton*, just as in early charters the names of the witnesses are regularly marked off from each other by full points placed either on the base-line or, like Greek colons, somewhat above it.

The next of the marks discussed in the Vallombrosa manuscript is the *interrogativus*. Direct questions cannot be expected to occur frequently in formal records, and when they are found in medieval documents they are as likely as not to lack any terminating mark of interrogation. The medieval scribe did, however, on occasion make use of a query which in design resembles a Greek colon surmounted by a semicircular arch. Care may be necessary to distinguish this sign from the superior mark of abbreviation (numbered 4 in the discussion above on p. 30) which stands for *ur*. In later writing the mark of interrogation is easily recognised.

The *periodus* of the Vallombrosa manuscript is a triangular arrangement of dots (∴)

[1] R. B. McKerrow: *Introduction to Bibliography* (Oxford, 2nd imp., 1928), p. 315.

' used at the end of a chapter or of a whole speech, when nothing further remains to be said '. Medieval English documents commonly dispense with any such sign of finality, and the *periodus* of later writers (used to conclude paragraphs as well as whole documents) was a combination of the point with the *virgula* (./).

The Vallombrosa manuscript describes the *semipunctus* as a point ' placed at the end of a line when it happens that a word is not completed there and continues on the following one '. When, in English documents of the 12th and 13th centuries, a word was broken at the end of a line and continued at the beginning of the next, it was quite usual for no mark of incompleteness to be inserted after the first part ; nor was the word divided according to any etymological or other principle. So far as division was governed by any rule at all it seems to have been that not less than two completing letters could be carried over to the second line. The medieval hyphen, when it does occur, is a long oblique stroke, often very lightly drawn and consequently easy to overlook. In later times formal documents on the whole avoid word-breaks, and spaces at the line's end too small to accommodate the whole of the word required are usually filled up with a flourish. Elsewhere the hyphen, still oblique, consists of two short parallel strokes like a tilted ' equals ' sign.

About the *gemipunctus*, as used in England, the Vallombrosa manuscript is certainly wrong. The *gemipunctus* consists of two full points placed horizontally on the base-line immediately before titles of dignity or office, thus : *reverendo in Christo patri* .. *Londoniensi episcopo*. (See Plate VIII.) These two points have been derived from those which commonly enclose an initial[1] (as it might be *reverendo in Christo patri* .J. *Londoniensi episcopo*) : the *gemipunctus*, it is supposed, is what is left when the initial is omitted, and is said by the Vallombrosa manuscript to be used ' for brevity's sake or to supply the place of a name we do not know '. There can, however, be no doubt that during the period of roughly two centuries (1250–1450[2]) in which the *gemipunctus* may be met in English documents it was honorific in intention and that English practice bears out the appropriateness of its German name of *Reverenzpunkt*. In numerous examples ignorance and the desire for brevity can be expressly excluded : as when the king of England speaks in 1283 of *clare memorie* .. *predecessoribus nostris* ;[3] or when the dean of Arches refers in 1325 to an incumbent as having been presented *per* .. *priorem et* .. *conventum Sancte Trinitatis London* ';[4] or, most strikingly of all, when a deed of 1311 contains the phrase *Walteri dei gracia Wigorniensis* .. *episcopi*.[5] A common editorial error of the past was the rendering of the *gemipunctus* in print by a succession of three or more dots, as if it indicated a lacuna.

In medieval manuscripts quoted matter and words not playing their ordinary part in the narrative (such as would nowadays appear in italics or between inverted commas) are sometimes enclosed in a sort of open-topped box, as in this example :

constat de interlineacione hujus verbi) predicti (in quinta linea.

In the 16th century round brackets, besides being used (rather more freely than they are used today) for enclosing parenthetical matter, are often given the function now allotted to inverted commas :

with this note in the mergyne (vacat).

---

[1] See above, p. 33.   [2] In domestic use it is most frequent between about 1300 and 1350.
[3] Anc. Correspondence 13/59.   [4] Anc. Deeds A. 12779.   [5] Univ. Coll. Oxon. Deeds MM1/2.

Modern stops not already mentioned are late in appearing in English manuscripts and may in most cases be assumed to have been introduced into this country by the printer.

Among the marks for which the reader should be on the alert are those which introduce paragraphs or mark off sub-headings from each other or from the text to which they relate. The commonest in medieval use in England are a ' gallows bracket ' derived ultimately from the Greek capital gamma, and an adaptation of the Latin capital C (originally representing *Capitulum*). The temptation is to try to see these marks as letters : indeed the second, which for a long time strongly resembles a doubled long *s*, was actually understood by later writers to be an abbreviation for *scilicet*. It is for this reason that even now some public notices and official documents which open with the name of a county will be found to continue with the mysterious words ' to wit '.

5

Errors and their Correction

The errors made by scribes fall into two groups : those they have left for us to detect, and those which they noticed and corrected themselves. The first group constitutes the field of textual criticism, which classifies the causes of scribal error and seeks to emend corrupt texts in ways that account for their corruptions. For various reasons archives offer only limited opportunities for the textual critic. Formal documents intended to be legally valid are inherently unlikely to contain serious errors, and the errors discoverable in most other kinds of archives normally comprise only a part of those possible in literary manuscripts, which may be several copies removed from their originals. The simple mistakes in copying which are to be found in archives are of the accidental nature to be explained by confusion between similar words, the substitution of the familiar and habitual for the unknown and unaccustomed, transposition, dittography (the writing twice what should have been written only once), haplography (the writing once what should have been written twice),[1] and other such perennial sources of error. Mishearing of dictated matter is sometimes advanced as a possible cause of scribal mistakes, but there is not much evidence to suggest that before quite modern times dictation entered at all significantly into the composition of English archives. From time to time, however, we can confidently ascribe a copyist's errors to the fact that he was transcribing a hand he could not read and making, *mutatis mutandis*, the same sort of mistakes as we make in those circumstances ourselves.

When the medieval scribe set out to correct the errors of omission and commission he had detected for himself, he followed certain conventions with which his modern reader should be familiar.

Erasure consists of the removal, with a sharp knife, of the surface bearing the matter to be deleted. It is a process obviously more suited to parchment, with its close texture and

---

[1] Both dittography and haplography are encouraged by homoeoteleuton, the presence in the original of two or more syllables, words, or phrases, ending in the same way, the copyist treating the second as if it were the first, or the first as if it were the second, occurrence of the duplicated ending. A simple example would be the rendering of *intendendo* as *intendendendo* (dittography) or *intendo* (haplography).

stout substance, than to paper.   The scraped surface was ' boned ' or polished with a piece of ivory, and the space filled either with a revised version of what had been erased or with a flourish or series of flourishes.   This new matter can often be recognised, because even thorough ' boning ' leaves the scraped surface more or less absorbent and ink applied to it is apt to spread slightly (Plate IV (b)).   Cancellation is a term properly applied to deletion by means of criss-cross lines (*cancelli* means ' lattice ' or ' trellis ') drawn across a whole passage ; but it is also applied to the crossing-out of individual words.   A method of deletion favoured by neat scribes, especially where the erroneous matter was not extensive, was to place dots below the unwanted letters, which are then said to be expunged. The number of dots does not seem to bear any constant relation to the number of letters intended to be affected ; some scribes place one dot below each letter they wish to delete, some are more lavish.   In the example illustrated in Plate III (b) below the scribe has made it clear that in one place the expunging dot deletes only a single minim of one letter.   Underlining as a means of deletion, which, though never common, is found from time to time in the later Middle Ages, may perhaps be a development from the practice of expunction. Obliteration usually takes the form of superimposing a correct letter on an incorrect one ; it has the disadvantage that it may sometimes be difficult for the reader to be sure (for example, in a proper name) which letter is meant to replace which.   Exceptionally obliteration may consist of the inking-out of erroneous matter.

Omissions are normally indicated by the caret familiar in modern manuscript, the omitted matter being inserted between the lines ; but where more material has to be added than can be conveniently interlined it is entered in the margin and distinguished by a mark or device of which a duplicate is drawn at the point of insertion.   These marks are very diverse in design and are occasionally quite elaborate.   Two thin oblique strokes (rather like acute accents) over each of two neighbouring words in a manuscript signify that the words are to be transposed in reading : examples are illustrated in Plates IV (a) and V (a) below.   The correct order, when dislocation has occurred, is sometimes suggested by the prefixing of the letters *a*, *b*, *c* to the words or phrases meant to be read first, second, and third.

Passages which it was desired to excise from continuous narrative are often enclosed between the two syllables of the word *vacat* (' it is void '), usually divided *va - cat* ; and this is quite often, as in the example shown in Plate IX (b), the sole indication that the passage has been deleted.   The normal method of invalidating the enrolment of a complete document or its entry in a register was by cancellation proper and the insertion in the margin of the word *vacat*, with a note of the reasons for, or the circumstances of, the cancellation.   From time to time it was necessary to invalidate an executed original. This was effected by folding it horizontally and making through the folded edge a series of cuts at an angle to it of about 45°.   When opened out the document thus bore across its face a number of ' herring-bone ' incisions, which were sufficient to destroy its legal effect without impairing its legibility.   Any seal it bore was removed.   There is one instance, probably unique, in the Public Records of the use of ' herring-bone ' cuts for cancelling an enrolment.   There are obvious reasons why the procedure should not have been applied to rolls.

CHAPTER V

ENGLISH HANDWRITING
FROM THE CONQUEST TO 1500

1

Hands in Use at the Conquest

The ancestry of the business hands used in England since the Norman Conquest might be traced to the origins of the alphabet, but it will perhaps be a sufficient introduction to the present survey to consider briefly the chief scripts with which the literate Englishman of the 11th century was familiar. In important Latin books of this period the ' displayed ' matter, consisting of titles, headings, sub-headings and exordia (the opening words of chapters, etc.), was likely to be shared between ' square ' and ' rustic ' capitals and uncials, while the body of the text was written in Carolingian minuscules, which had fairly recently displaced half-uncials as the standard Latin-language book hand of the Saxons. For works in English the native insular minuscules were employed. Examples of these six hands are illustrated in Plate I.

Square capitals, which had been used in the 4th century (and perhaps earlier) for the composition of entire texts, are of essentially the same form as the ' roman ' capital alphabet of the modern printer ; they simulate in manuscript the carved inscriptional style of which Trajan's Column provides a fine and famous example. The name ' square ' (*quadrata*), which is at least as old as Petronius,[1] is due to their proportion, since they are all (at any rate in principle) of one height and almost all either as wide or half as wide as they are high, so that each can be contained fairly exactly within a square or half-square. The posture and pen-hold necessary to execute these characters in manuscript and to reproduce the serifs[2] of the inscriptional prototype were unnatural and tiring ; and the progress of the scribe writing, or rather lettering, in square capitals must have been very slow.

Rustic capitals were conspicuously better suited to the materials and instruments of writing. Modelled originally on the freehand lettering of the painted signboard, they are taller and narrower in proportion than square capitals, of which, nevertheless, they are only a more negligently and economically written form. The dominance of the pen in determining their design is apparent in the angle of shading and in the slight sagging curve imparted to those oblique strokes which in *quadrata* are straight. Serifs, especially foot-serifs, are fairly consistently preserved ; and their presence, coupled with the narrowness

---

[1] *Satyricon*, 29 : *canis ingens catena vinctus in pariete erat pictus, superque quadrata littera scriptum* CAVE CANEM.

[2] The short cross-lines at the extremities of the main strokes. They are sometimes said to have originated through the necessity, for technical reasons, of finishing off in this way letters incised in stone with the V-shaped chisel.

of the characters, creates the need for differentiating between easily confused letters. The narrow *F*, with its foot-serif as long as its arms, could be readily mistaken for *E*, as could *I* for *L*; and to distinguish between these pairs scribes extend *F* and *L* above the headline.[1] Confusion between *I* and *T* is avoided by omitting, or merely suggesting, the head-serif of *I*. Rustic *A* has no crossbar, and the foot-serif of the thinner left-hand stroke curves inwards to meet the heavy right-hand stroke, which projects slightly at the top.

What style of calligraphy, if any, St. Jerome had in mind when he wrote in his Preface to Job about *éditions de luxe* executed in *unciales litterae*, must remain uncertain, since in their context the words can refer only to size.[2] But in modern usage (dating from the 18th century) ' uncial ' is the name given to the distinctive book hand which was extensively employed for sacred Christian texts in Latin between the 5th and 8th centuries. In general appearance uncials are open and round : the test-letters *A, D, E, H, M* all substitute curves for original angles. Of the other letters, *B, C, I, N, O, R, S, T* and *X* retain to a greater or less extent their square-capital form and alignment, and the rest (notably *F, G* and *Q*, which have all become descenders) suffer some modification of them.

The three hands so far discussed are known collectively as majuscules. What they have in common is not so much the large size that this name might suggest (indeed, rustic capitals are often written quite small), as the fact that each has few or very few extruding characters, that is, characters which ascend above the upper, or descend beneath the lower, of two horizontal parallels. It is for this reason that half-uncials, in which ascenders and descenders are more numerous, are usually grouped with the minuscules or ' four-line ' scripts. In half-uncial, *a* is single-bowled, *b* and *d* normally ascend perpendicularly, *g* is a descender with a horizontal head and frequently resembles some later forms of *z*, *l* has a rounded foot, and the uprights of *m* are parallel. The angular ' capital ' *N* survives, its cross-stroke often nearly horizontal ; but in the characteristic *R* of half-uncial the bow is not brought fully round to meet the descending perpendicular, and the vestigial tail is parallel to the base-line. In half-uncial, *s* takes the ' long ' form.[3]

The distinctively ' insular ' type of half-uncial which formed the Saxons' book hand had originated in Ireland, where side by side with it there had been evolved a small, condensed, upright minuscule, used for glosses. Its affinities with the native half-uncial are most conspicuous in the serifs common to both styles. It is these sharp-wedged serifs which confer its distinctive pointed appearance on the insular minuscule.

On the continent of Europe experiment and reform carried on for the greater part of the 8th century produced the text hand we now know as Carolingian minuscule (Plate I (a)), with which the name of Alcuin of York is intimately associated. The characters of this minuscule are recognisably the models for the ' lower-case ' roman letters used in the printing of this book ; only the long *s* and the curved non-ascending *t* qualify the essential ' modernity ' of the alphabet. The Danish invasions of the 9th century post-

[1] This practice is admittedly to be found also in square-capital writing, where the need for it is not equally obvious.

[2] The passage runs : *veteres libros vel in membranis purpureis auro argentoque descriptos vel uncialibus, ut vulgo aiunt, litteris onera magis exarata quam codices.* The natural interpretation of this is ' in inch-high letters, as the saying goes ' ; but ' letters twelve to the line ' has also been suggested. It is difficult to believe that *ut vulgo aiunt* apologises for the use of a *technical* term.

[3] Not all these features are to be seen in the ' insular ' half-uncial illustrated in Plate I (b), which is thought by some scholars to be classifiable as a majuscule.

poned the date at which this continental reform began powerfully to influence Saxon practice, but during the 10th century the characteristic insular style began to lose ground to Carolingian in literary, liturgical, and documentary use and to be increasingly confined to writing in the vernacular.   Yet even in the 11th century, when the orthodox Carolingian hand, written according to the continental rules,[1] may be said to be fairly established in England, a diploma (or land-charter) whose Latin text is in pure Carolingian will often be found to have the vernacular description of the boundaries in the insular hand.   Not only so, but native proper names, whether in English or latinised form, occurring in the middle of the Latin text are also written in the insular alphabet.   This appropriation of specific styles to specific languages is a recurring phenomenon in the history of English writing.

2

The Emergence of Archive Hands

The English had never cultivated an official or business hand such as those which, derived ultimately from Roman cursive, were practised on the Continent ; and at the Conquest any Latin text written in England, whether literary, liturgical, or legal, was as likely as any other to reflect the pervasiveness of the Carolingian reforms.   Thus the text of Domesday Book itself is in a clear Carolingian minuscule and its headings and displayed matter in rustic capitals.

The usual division of post-Conquest English writing is into ' book ' and ' charter ' hands, the first characterised by their use in literary and liturgical manuscripts and the second by their use in business documents.   But for some time after the Conquest the difference in function induced no significant difference of form.   The writers of literary manuscripts were catering for a widely dispersed class of learned readers : they were at the same time more susceptible to influences exerted on the literate world as a whole and more concerned to conserve and standardise their practices than the writers of business documents intended for a limited and local audience.   The development of the post-Conquest book hand is therefore to a great extent common to many countries, certainly to those of northern Europe, rather than a purely English phenomenon.   The direction of this development can be seen to be due to the desire to save space without sacrifice of dignity.   North of the Alps this was achieved by the evolution of a closer-set, narrower minuscule than the Carolingian original, and to it weight and solidity were added by the use of a broader pen.   A narrow letter executed with a broad pen must inevitably have its curves replaced by angles : and the angular appearance of the book hand was yet further emphasised by lozenge-shaped serifs placed obliquely to the heads (and in one style also to the feet) of perpendicular strokes.   By about 1200 the book-hand minuscule had substantially taken the form which it was to retain (with a steady increase in massiveness) until the 15th century, when it was transferred, just as it was, to the types of the first printers. The resemblance of a page written in this style to a woven pattern (*textus*) is responsible

---

[1] For ' capital ' initials needed in the body of the text Alcuin had used uncial forms, but by the 11th century rustic capitals were more usual.

for the name ' text hand ' by which many scholars would prefer it to be called.   The calligraphers of the Renaissance coined for it the contemptuous epithet ' gothic ', which they
used in the same sense of ' barbarous ' as Sir Christopher Wren describing the Early English,
Decorated, and Perpendicular styles of architecture.

The additional weight to which the minuscule had been subjected by the broad pen
could not be similarly imposed on the slender rustic capitals, which were gradually abandoned during the 12th century in favour of a rounded capital of something like uncial
form.   Already at the time of Domesday Book an *H* and an *M* of uncial pattern had established themselves in the rustic capital alphabet, and the four-stroke *E* was being frequently
varied by a round quasi-uncial one.   By the end of the 12th century these forms were
supplemented by uncial *U* with a foot-serif on the right, a cabriole-legged *N*, and a *T* with
a curved shank (the last two owing something to the design of their minuscule counterparts) ;
and all were freely used as optional variants even in matter written in *quadrata*.[1]   To give
them prominence and to bring them into harmony with the text letter, book scribes built
up these rounded capitals with broad and solid strokes and at the same time extended
and exaggerated their serifs, so that the arms of *E*, for example, or the feet of *M* are linked
by a continuous curved line.

The relevance of the text hand to the study of manuscript archives does not lie only
in the common origin of text and business hands in England and their virtual identity during
an important period.   Until the Renaissance, text provided for the overwhelming majority
of readers the norm or standard by which legibility was judged, and thus influenced the
reforms and limited the innovations introduced into business writing.

3

Characteristics of the earlier Business Hands

Almost all the English archives now surviving from the century or so following the
Conquest are of a more or less ceremonious character and therefore may not reflect
accurately the rate at which business writing as a whole developed away from the literary
hand.   But by about 1150 at the latest it is possible to say that certain features are common
to the work of clerks whose normal employment is on business documents.   The perpendicularly ascending *d* of the orthodox text hand has been definitively replaced by a
form in which the ascender is bent backwards, and the stem of *r* descends well below the
base-line.   The serifs of the literary minuscule are passing imperceptibly, in business writing,
into the ' ties ' between strokes or letters which assist speed and fluency.   The rounding
of capitals offered similar assistance and was quickly taken up (perhaps in some cases,
such as *T*, actually introduced) by the writers of archives.   The broad strokes and fattened
curves of the text-hand capitals were represented in business writing in outline, as it were,
by the addition to the characters of internal lines paralleling the main straight strokes and
forming chords to the rounded ones.

When, at the end of the 12th century, we are able to consult informal business writing

---

[1] They give its distinctive character to the capital alphabet (sometimes called ' Lombardic ') used
from about 1175 until the middle of the 14th century for the lettering on English seals.

—in the earliest Plea Rolls, for example, or in the enrolments, as opposed to the sealed engrossments, of royal charters—we find a style which argues a fairly long tradition of rapid cursive. Engrossments under the Great Seal are still written with a certain deliberation and some regard for the separate formation of individual letters ; the enrolments exhibit the same letters, formed in the same way, but present them in a smaller size and with no attempt to disguise the frankly cursive character of the writing. There is, however, as yet no distinction between the *hands* used for business purposes ; such difference as can be detected is between the ceremonious and the workaday employment of a single style.

During the 13th century the contrast between text and business hands became more marked. It was still possible for a pure text hand to be used for archives : the Salisbury exemplar of Magna Carta is written in a more than passable book hand ; and the hands used for private charters between about 1220 and 1240 often have strong affinities with contemporary text.[1] But in general the hands used for archives were developing along the lines suggested by the early divergence between the ceremonious and the less so.[2] Writers soon evolved cursive forms of the uncialised capitals—forms which encompassed the basic design, the serifs, and the adventitious internal lines in the fewest possible actions of the pen. The long-stemmed *r* had become virtually universal in archives (though both text and business hands used the Arabic-2 form of *r* after round-bodied letters). The minuscules *b, h, k,* and *l* now begin with a small hook on the right of the ascender ; and as the century proceeds this hook approximates more and more, in informal writing, to a loop. On the opposite (left-hand) side of the ascenders of these letters there appears, about midway through the century, a curved, spur-like projection which in the course of the next fifty years is found progressively higher up the vertical stroke, reaching the top (where it duplicates symmetrically the hook on the right) about 1300 and subsequently disappearing. Towards the end of the century long *s* ceases to be written in the final position ; and the ' beaver-tailed ' capital *S* (so often since that time misread as *M*) enjoys its comparatively brief vogue. While text remains rigidly upright, the business hands of the 13th century will often be found to exhibit a slight backward slope. But by the time of Edward I the archive hand is normally regular and upright, with short extruders[3] and little space between the lines. The contrast between thick and thin strokes is more marked than at any previous time : the distinctive appearance of the hand is, indeed, largely due to the weight given to the longer perpendiculars and to the diagonal stroke which completes the looped ascender of *d.*

Under Edward II the loss of the left-hand hook from the ascenders of *b, h, k,* and *l,* and the increasingly frequent appearance of a loop on the left of the descending strokes of *f, p,* and long *s* create an appearance of growing speed and currency in execution ; though

---

[1] Late examples of the literary hand in non-ceremonious archive contexts include a Lincolnshire jury panel of 1250 (Chancery Files, A.1) and a number of entries in a Channel Islands Eyre Roll of 1323–4 (Assize Rolls, etc., 1165, mm. 13 and 14).

[2] A 15th-century critic of a charter purporting to speak from the reign of Henry III condemns it as a forgery, among other reasons because ' the writing is a kind of text or set hand (*litera est quasi textus sive sethonde*), and there was no such manner of writing of old time ' (Historical MSS. Commission, Eighth Report, 1881 (re-issued 1908), App. 1 (II), No. 265b).

[3] The exaggerated lengthening and thickening of the ascenders in the top line of a document is a modest form of embellishment which lasted for centuries.

the typical business hand of this period remains an orderly and eminently legible cursive, which, at its own level, is not without calligraphic pretensions. But from about 1330 there is a steady decline in regularity and architectural quality : even in formal documents the writing is not only strongly cursive but wanting in discipline, and suggests an unsuccessful attempt to reconcile the claims of ceremoniousness and speed.

4

Bastard

It is at this time, with English business handwriting ripe for reform, that we first hear of a body of men called *scriptores litere curialis*, the writers of the ' court letter ', or scriveners.[1] (*Litera curialis*, translated by ' court letter ' or ' court hand ', has the entirely general meaning of handwriting used to record any kind of business transaction, as opposed to the book hand : it embraces, but is by no means restricted to, the hands written in courts of justice.[2]) It would be natural for a young profession to welcome new technical developments and to seek the means of distinguishing its work from that of the uninitiated ; and it may well be that the scriveners played an important part in the reform of English business handwriting which followed upon the introduction of the bastard hand into this country in the second half of the 14th century.

Bastard, as its name[3] implies, is a hybrid : it combines some of the features of the canonical text hand with some of the elements of cursive writing. Whatever the shame attaching to its genesis, it rapidly achieved an independent position of its own in the widening gap between the formal text, used for first-class literary and liturgical manuscripts in Latin, and the unambitious archive hands, and in one or another of its forms it was widely written all over Europe. For the vernacular literatures it provided a medium consistent with their increasing dignity ; in business documents it had the advantage of being more speedily written than text and more legible and more professional-looking than any contemporary cursive. By the earliest known English writing masters, who belong to the 16th century, this hand was known as ' bastard secretary '—an unfortunate name in so far as it suggests that it is a form, and not the ancestor, of the secretary hand.

Written in England over a period of at least two hundred years and by scribes of every degree of competence, bastard naturally varies perceptibly between writer and writer and from date to date (Plates XI (b) to XIII). The general characteristics may be summed up as uprightness and angularity, both inherited from text, and a certain discretion in the use of ' ties ', or linking-strokes. The angularity is due to the same causes, and is brought about by the same means, as had formerly produced the characteristic appearance of text :

[1] By 1357 the London scriveners were already organised into a gild, whose members were in that year exempted from jury service. See H. T. Riley : *Memorials of London . . . in the XIIIth, XIVth and XVth Centuries* (1868), p. 295.

[2] Cf. the use on the Continent of *notula curiensis* in the same sense, noticed below, p. 61*n.*

[3] On the historicity of the name see Hilary Jenkinson : *The Later Court Hands in England* (Cambridge, 1927), p. 14.

the letters are laterally compressed and what had originally been curves are 'broken'[1] into angles.   With few exceptions the serifs of text are absent from bastard, which achieves a look of pointedness by means of a terminal tapering of the perpendiculars which is particularly noticeable in descenders like *p* and *q*.   The earliest English examples of bastard borrow the text forms of *d*, *g*, and *r* (the last with its foot-serif), but by the end of the 14th century the old cursive (looped) *d*, the reversed *e*, and the long-stemmed descending *r* are creeping back into use ; and the text-type *r* has assumed a cursive form in which the right of the foot-serif is joined to the top of the main stroke.

Bastard is best regarded as the family name for a number of hands rather than as a precise appellation for one.   The 15th-century writing masters of France and Germany confined the name, and its synonym *brevitura*, to a single species, but it is well to remember that they had a professional interest in swelling the number of hands they were prepared to teach.   It was, in any case, impossible that a style in almost universal use would everywhere retain its schoolroom orthodoxy.

5

Fifteenth-century 'Free' Hands

Among the effects exerted on handwriting by the invention of printing mention has already been made of the typographical fixation of text at the stage it had then reached. But the spread of printing inevitably killed the demand for manuscript books ; and the talents of calligraphers were diverted into other fields, notably that of teaching.   At the same time the hands practised for business purposes found themselves thrust into a position in which they began to set the calligraphic standard instead of conforming, however imperfectly, to it.   It is thus no accident that the rise and development of the special set hands associated with the departments of the central government in England are roughly contemporaneous with the emergence of the printer and the writing master.   At the beginning of this period bastard was established as the orthodox hand for all ceremonious business purposes ; and the departments were evolving, with varying rapidity, the distinctive styles whose matured characteristics are discussed in the next chapter.

Elsewhere bastard was developing in a more haphazard fashion.   The number of 'free', highly personalised correspondence hands practised in England during the second half of the 15th century is bewilderingly large.   With more or less of bastard, and less or more of the old cursives, in their composition they almost all defy classification (Plate XIV (b)).   But one late-15th-century modification of bastard is worthy of attention as the hand upon which the characteristic style of the following century or so was founded. This is the hand described by Sir Hilary Jenkinson as 'splayed', which has certain affinities with the *lettre de minute* taught in France, side by side with bastard, about the middle of the 15th century (Plate XII (b)).   The characteristic English form is a small hand with the appearance of vertical compression : the minims composing *i*, *m*, *n*, and *u* have a pronounced backward slope, while the 'ties', or linking strokes, have a fully compensating slope to the right.   The effect, especially noticeable in words like *annuum* or *minimum*,

---

[1] Hence the name '*fractura*', given to both bastard and text.

is to produce a series of alternate slopes, or baseless isosceles triangles, reminiscent of the teeth of a saw. Descenders, which are generally short, have a progressively more marked slope. The hand has what a modern typographer would call low x-height : that is to say that letters like *a*, *c*, and *o*, which do not ascend or descend, are vertically compressed and ' splayed ' by comparison with the original bastard. The appearance of smallness is largely illusory, in that there is no gain in the amount of written matter to the line. Distinctive letter-forms are *e*, *g*, *t* (which is readily distinguishable from *c* through the lengthening of the main stroke above the cross), *x* (which by the end of the century is being written in one continuous stroke of the pen), *p* (also written in one action, virtually the same as that for *x*, with consequent assimilation), and *r* (which is normally of the text type, linking the foot-serif to the head of the main stroke, but may take the Arabic-2 shape in any position).

CHAPTER VI

ENGLISH HANDWRITING SINCE 1500

1

Secretary Hands

Whether the effect of the Renaissance was actually to increase literacy in England or merely to discredit a medieval view that writing might be within a gentleman's capacity while remaining beneath his dignity, the later years of the 15th century mark the beginning of the decline of the formal document as the sole, or even the chief, written product of English administration. The processes which culminate in the formal instrument are increasingly well documented ; new types of business, and a great volume of that hitherto conducted orally, find written expression ; and the principals in most transactions are literate of necessity. The diversity of the uses to which writing was now put demanded, and ultimately produced, a universally acceptable style—one which could be written quickly and read everywhere without difficulty—a handwriting for the ordinary man.

The earliest direct evidence for the activity of the English writing master is the printed book of instruction, *A Booke containing Divers Sortes of Hands*, published in 1571[1] by Jean de Beauchesne and John Baildon. There is evidence, however, that there existed on the Continent in the 15th and early 16th centuries a class of itinerant teachers of writing ;[2] and from the surviving fragments of their advertisements and specimen-books it seems clear that there was some demand in France and Germany for instruction in the hands employed in everyday life. It is reasonable to suppose that a similar demand was made and met in England, and that the writing master was exerting considerable influence in England for at least a generation before the appearance of the Beauchesne and Baildon book. This influence seems to have been in the direction of systematising and standardising the tendencies observable in the ' splayed ' and cognate hands of the period, so that devices originally representing the short cuts and economies of individuals were canonised and incorporated into the orthodox hand taught under the name of secretary (Plates XVII (a), XIX (b), XX (a)).

It was inevitable that a hand having such mixed origins should display many different subtypes and that the writing master's natural desire to increase his apparent range should do nothing to reduce the number. Martin Billingsley, himself a writing master, complains that ' to speake of the kindes of Secretary is (in these dayes) no easie matter : for some have devised so many, and those so strange and disguised, that there is hardly any true straine of a right Secretary in them. For mine own part I make distinction between the Sett,

---

[1] One surviving copy bears the publication date 1570.
[2] See S. H. Steinberg : ' Medieval Writing-Masters ', in *The Library*, Series IV, Vol. XXI (1941), pp. 1–24.

Facill, and Fast hands.' [1]   Billingsley's three main types of secretary seem to correspond to those more descriptively named, by Sir Hilary Jenkinson, ' engrossing ', ' upright ', and ' sloped '.   The ' true straine of a right Secretary ' in these three is disclosed by their common possession of a number of letter-forms, of which the following may be selected as characteristic.

The letter *e*, though often in the ' reversed ' form, is most commonly reminiscent of the Greek minuscule epsilon in one of the forms familiar to us in recent printing.   It is occasionally close in appearance to *c*, which consists normally of two strokes, a short perpendicular and a horizontal projecting from it.   One of the test-letters of secretary is *h*, which concludes with a steeply descending leftward curve (rarely varied by a descending loop) ; and ligatures comprising *h* and preceding *g*, *s*, and *t* are very common.   As in the splayed hand, *p* is written in one continuous action of the pen and can seldom be distinguished in form from *x*.   The orthodox secretary *r* is the two-stemmed type evolved from the cursive rendering of the seriffed bastard-text character, but the Arabic-2 variety is also admissible in any position.   The letters *a*, *c*, and *g* are sometimes begun with a long straight stroke, inclined to the right and rising high above the line of writing (Plate XIX (b)) ; and foot-serifs are occasionally given to *l* and *t*, and less often to *p*.

When secretary emerges as a distinctive hand, towards the middle of the 16th century the only style practised is the upright ; and it was another generation before the writing masters added to it a style deliberately inclined in the interests of more rapid execution. The slope is at first by no means consistent as between different letters : the descenders of double-*f* and double-*s* almost always diverge sharply, and capital *A* is often given a pronounced backward slope.   But from the time of its introduction the sloped style was influenced by the consistent slope exhibited by the italic hand.   Engrossing secretary (Plate XX (b)), which is essentially a ceremonious hand, is interesting as illustrating the extent to which the writing masters were able, by means of calligraphic polishing, to raise a utilitarian hand to a standard of regularity in design which will bear comparison with any of the set hands practised contemporaneously with it.   Its chief characteristics are a conspicuous and really consistent uprightness, the almost complete absence of linking-strokes between the letters,[2] and a marked contrast between the firm main-strokes and the hair-lines of the subsidiary ones.   That there should have been room for another ceremonious hand is evidence of the importance of the vernacular in business and administration, since secretary is *par excellence* the vehicle for matter in English.   The abbreviations evolved centuries before to shorten the labour of writing Latin were of greatly diminished value to the writer in the vernacular : some of them he could, and did, use, but others were either unsuitable or unintelligible.   Speed was now achieved rather by more rapid execution than by a system of selective omission ; and the characteristic ligatures of secretary are those which arise naturally from the frequent writing of common English letter-combinations.

[1] Martin Billingsley : *A Coppie Book containing . . . Examples of all the most Curious Hands* (2nd edn., 1637).

[2] For this reason it was the obvious model for contemporary printing-types which set out to simulate manuscript.

2

Humanistic Hands

From the earliest days of the Italian Renaissance its leaders entertained a lively admiration for the Carolingian minuscule in which many of their newly recovered manuscripts were written. With this admiration went an equally lively distaste for the literary hands of their own time,[1] and it was therefore not long before attempts were made to revive or imitate the Carolingian style. By the opening years of the 15th century scribes employed by the humanists were writing a formal upright seriffed minuscule, based on the Carolingian model and called by contemporaries the *litera antiqua*, or, in Italian, *antica*. It was this hand, matured over the next fifty years and supplemented by an 'inscriptional' capital alphabet, which determined the form of the 'roman' types with which printing has made the modern reader familiar. A cursive, slightly inclined version of the humanistic minuscule was evolved during the first half of the 15th century and was adopted about 1450 in the papal Chancery[2] for the writing of those documents, less formal than bulls, which are known as 'briefs'.

The challenge of the upright *antica* was to the contemporary book hands: it was hardly to be expected that a style requiring so much time and skill from the writer would be adopted for any of the purposes of business. In the event, when once the printer had succeeded in reproducing it in type, the demand for the upright manuscript *antica*, even in the literary field, inevitably faded away. The humanistic cursive, however, which had developed in the papal Chancery into a disciplined and regular hand, was taken up by the leaders of taste and fashion, among whom it soon became the normal vehicle for private correspondence in Latin.

The humanistic hands were appreciated in England before 1500, though it is probable that the printer did more than the scribe to familiarise English readers with the upright roman. The credit for introducing the cursive italic into this country is traditionally given to Peters Carmelianus, Henry VII's Latin secretary, who followed continental precedent by reserving it for material in Latin. The English themselves observed no strict rule of this kind. The cursive italic, known by this time (somewhat confusingly) as 'roman', appears in English archives with growing frequency after the first third of the 16th century. Its use in the signatures appended to letters written in secretary is common from about 1550. Quoted matter (whether in Latin or not) occurring in the middle of a document written in secretary is usually distinguished by being in italic, which is also often introduced for headings and marginalia. But it was as an alternative to secretary for all purposes, rather than as a supplement for some, that italic was admitted to general use in England. School statutes of the 16th and early 17th centuries prescribe the teaching of the 'roman' and secretary hands in terms which suggest a parity of esteem. There was never any question of the elevation of italic into the status of a special 'set' hand: it had reached England as

---

[1] In a letter of 1366 to Boccaccio, Petrarch refers to the writers, 'or rather painters', of their day who practised, 'as if it had been invented for some other purpose than to be read, a rambling and florid hand, charming when viewed from a distance but at close quarters trying and fatiguing to the eyes' (*Epist. Fam.* XXIII).

[2] Hence its contemporary Italian name of *cancellaresca* (*corsiva*), variously translated by modern historians of italic handwriting.

a correspondence hand, and its use in this country, as early as the reign of Henry VIII, for matter in the vernacular[1] gives a fairly clear indication of the function it was to serve here. By 1600 it was being written with such a magnificent disregard for any calligraphical rules that it might be illegible to the writer's contemporaries and compatriots.[2]

3

Emergence of the Round Hand

When two structurally different hands are taught simultaneously and employed without distinction for general purposes, mutual borrowings are likely to produce, sooner or later, a hybrid style possessing reminiscences of both. The first twenty years of the 17th century provide numerous English examples of the influence exerted on each other by secretary and italic ; and for the next generation there is an uninterrupted increase in the occurrence of ' mixed ' hands about which it is difficult to decide whether they should be called secretary powerfully affected by italic, or italic with many secretary features (Plate XXI (b)). Towards the end of the century the fusion of the two hands was canonised by the writing masters (notably ' Colonel ' John Ayres) as the English national round hand, in which was discernible the influence of the *italienne-bastarde* illustrated by the Frenchman, Lucas Materot of Avignon, in the copy-book he published in 1608.

Early in the 18th century the English adopted generally the modern distinction, already established in French practice, between *i* and *j*, and *u* and *v* ; and in the course of the next fifty years the round hand, with an increased rightward slope and provided with loops for the ascenders of *b*, *f*, *h*, *k*, and *l*, and the descenders of *f*, *g*, *j*, *y*, and *z*, took on the appearance with which we are still familiar today. The superior speed and businesslike aspect of this hand commended it to foreign writing schools and it soon spread over most of the Continent. In France, Spain, and even Italy, it achieved a position, never since seriously threatened, only just short of the pre-eminence it has enjoyed for two and a half centuries in this country.

The form of the round hand has until our own time changed so little that the rest of its story is soon told. The 19th century produced the ' Carstairs system ' [3] (which sought to increase speed by involving the whole forearm, and not merely the fingers, in the action of writing) and the fine steel pen. Writing became thinner and lighter ; the contrast between fine up-strokes and thicker down-strokes was gratuitously emphasised and exaggerated, and the rightward slope was increased.

There are some interesting comments by Palmerston, as Home Secretary, in a minute of 1854,[4] on the specimens of handwriting submitted to him in consequence of his publicly

---

[1] Sir Hilary Jenkinson (*The Later Court Hands in England*, Plate XXVII (vii)) illustrates a petition in English, dated 1535. For an even earlier example of a humanistic hand for the vernacular see Augmentation Office, Misc. Books, 31/100, a typical Latin and English bond, dated 1521.

[2] In State Papers Domestic, James I, 52/56, John Daniel describes Essex's love-letters as ' written in such a ragged romane hand ' that he could not read them.

[3] Joseph Carstairs (*fl.* 1797–1820) exerted a powerful influence abroad, especially in America.

[4] Home Office Records, ' O.S.' Papers, 5280 and 5540.

expressed criticisms of contemporary hands and methods of teaching. He himself preferred the styles of the beginning and middle of the 18th century, and deplored the contrast between thick and thin strokes and the appearance of what he calls 'a series of parrallel lines' in Victorian writing.[1]

The reaction against this style, begun by reformers like William Morris, belongs rather to the history of aesthetics than to that of English business handwriting, since few of the hands devised by the reformers have contributed significantly to the making of English archives. In the age of the typewriter it is doubtful whether they ever will.

4

The distinctive Departmental Hands

Differentiation between the set, or departmental, hands practised in England is not very easy in the formative stages of their development; the nearer they are in date to their common ancestor, the bastard hand of the early 15th century, the less likely they are to exhibit the characteristics which later mark them off from one another. The discussion which follows will therefore be directed to the established or typical forms of each.

The best-known and most easily recognised of the departmental hands is that practised in the royal Chancery at Westminster and for Chancery-type business in the three palatinates. This hand will be met in all instruments under the Great Seal, such as the engrossments of royal letters patent and original writs, and in the long and numerous series of Chancery enrolments. Its origin has been placed as early as the reign of Henry VI, but there is no evidence that it was recognised as a distinctive hand as soon as this. Writing to John Paston in 1454, John Clopton refers to his letter as 'wretyn with my chauncery hand, in ryth gret haste',[2] using the term, as can be seen from the manuscript, in the sense in which it was understood on the Continent, as a generic description of a 'court' or business hand.[3] When Stephen Gardiner refers in 1547 to 'the chancery hande',[4] it is clear that he means that written in the English Chancery, but Gardiner had been Chancellor himself and in his day the chief characteristics of the Chancery hand had been established for about two generations.

The general impression conveyed by this hand (Plates XIV (a), XVIII) is one of roundness, the roundness of any one letter being effected by a number of constituent, but by no means concentric, arcs. The characters are upright and almost all 'wide-set', with generous lateral spacing. The orthodox *r* is of the descending, long-stemmed type common in 15th-century bastard and is not, in the fully developed chancery style, linked to the following letter. The Arabic-2 form of *r* is used after *o* and *a* but not after any other

---

[1] An exasperated civil servant has marked one of the letters enclosing a specimen: 'Is the Secretary of State dwindled down into a Writing-Master?'

[2] James Gairdner (ed.): *The Paston Letters* (Edinburgh, 1910), Vol. I, p. 285.

[3] The bilingual advertisement of Johann Brune, a German writing master (*fl.* 1490–1510), seems to use *cancelleysch* to translate *notula curiensis prout communiter scribitur in curiis . . . principum.* See *The Library*, Series IV, Vol. XXI, p. 19.

[4] J. A. Muller: *Letters of Stephen Gardiner* (Cambridge, 1933), p. 275, citing Foxe.

round-bodied letter except in some engrossments, which may also illustrate the x-height *r* of text.   In the earliest form of the style the links between minims are very faintly indicated at the base and subsequently disappear altogether, the process encouraging the lateral compression which makes *m*, *n*, and *u* the only prominent exceptions to the rule that the characters are wide-set.   Ascenders are commonly short but there is less contraction of descenders, which do not preserve the taper that characterises earlier bastard.   There is a growing tendency, as time goes on, for the marks of contraction and suspension above abbreviated words to become conventionalised : a very thin horizontal dash, varied in some positions or by some scribes by a short curved one, is made to do duty for almost all the superior marks of abbreviation.   But conventionalisation of some such kind is common to all the later court hands and is perhaps to be seen rather as a sign of declining Latinity in the writer than of deliberate policy in his instructors.

The clerks of the Exchequer contributed comparatively little to the writing of documents now to be found outside official custody, so that the Exchequer hands are of interest primarily to the student of the public records.   The standard authority[1] on post-1500 handwriting in England distinguishes three Exchequer hands, associated respectively with the King's (Queen's) Remembrancer's and the Lord Treasurer's Remembrancer's departments and the Pipe Office.   The first two may be regarded as together occupying a position, with respect to their design, midway between the Chancery hand and the common-law (or legal) hand, with the King's Remembrancer's hand approximating more closely to the Chancery style and the Lord Treasurer's Remembrancer's to the legal.

The chief characteristics of the K.R. hand (Plate XXIII) can be summarised as follows. Slight departures from the generally vertical towards right or left, together with a certain squatness in the minuscules, produce a sprawling appearance.   There is no avoidance of links between letters or minims ; indeed the wide angle at which the foot of descending *r* is carried up to join the following letter is one of the distinctive features of the hand.   The angles of bastard are retained or revived where the Chancery hand has softened them into curves.   Distinctive letter-forms are displayed by *g* (which is much narrower-waisted than the Arabic-8 form of the Chancery hand and often has its lower bowl uncompleted on the right), reversed *e* (often difficult to distinguish from *d*, which, with a very short ascender, is written in an identical action), and *t* (taller than in the Chancery hand and coming to a point at the top).

So far as the formation of individual letters is concerned, the L.T.R. hand (Plate XXII) differs from this only in normally avoiding reversed *e* and having a typical *r* of the Arabic-2 form, but its general appearance, which is quite distinctive, is produced by extreme lateral compression of the letters accompanied, for once, by no increase in angularity.

The hand practised in the Pipe Office (Plate XXI (a)) is perhaps the only Exchequer hand at all likely to be met often in documents in private ownership.   The Pipe Roll itself had always been written, from the earliest times, with an obvious regard for ceremoniousness and dignity : and long tradition reinforced the respect in which it had been held since the 12th century as the principal record of the sovereign's dealings with his debtors.   The influences which produced the other departmental hands introduced comparatively few peculiarities into the already large and bold Pipe Office hand.   These peculiarities are

---

[1] Sir Hilary Jenkinson's *The Later Court Hands in England.*

most noticeable in the matter which is given special prominence by being written extra large : only the head and foot serifs of minims are written, the perpendicular stroke itself disappears ; and fanciful forms, suggesting the most irrelevant *chinoiserie*, are devised for the capital *S* of *Summa* (an important recurring word in the Pipe Roll), and occasionally for *Et*, in the formula *Et quietus est*.

By ' court hand ' the later writing masters primarily understood the hand written in the records of the courts of Common Pleas and King's (Queen's) Bench. It was not, however, confined to such records, being extensively used by lawyers and their clerks not only for documents such as deeds, etc., but for such purposes as personal memoranda and commonplace books. The essential forms of the characters are the same in all the varying sizes in which the hand is written, but its cursiveness diminishes with increasing size. The chief peculiarities of this hand (Plates XIX (a), XXVI, XXIX) are as follows. It is conspicuously upright (though late and degenerate examples often show a backward slope) and laterally compressed, with exaggeratedly long ascenders and descenders, the latter often, and the former sometimes, brought round in sweeping crescent-shaped curves. The internal strokes[1] which still characterise the ' gothic ' capitals have developed in *C, E, G,* and *Q* a wedge-shaped form which in early examples descends but in later times ascends some distance above the letter. Strongly characteristic letters are *a, p, e, g, t,* and *i* in the final position, where it carries an appendage like a squirrel's tail.

The departmental set hands were all the products of a more or less self-conscious search for distinctiveness. This fact alone would have prevented them, or any one of them, from setting standards of utility and legibility ; and their use for the most formal purposes was bound to result in their being written almost exclusively by a relatively small, and relatively humble, class of specialist clerks and copyists. Their highly mannered style was completely divorced from the circumstances of everyday life, and though the tradition which kept them in being was carefully fostered by those who taught and practised them, it is clear that by the middle of the 17th century they had come to be regarded as part of the apparatus of professional mystification. When, in 1650, the Commonwealth legislators sought to establish English as the only official language for all domestic administrative purposes,[2] they expelled, at the same time as Latin, the departmental set hands with which alone, or almost alone, the use of Latin was by this time associated. Records of all kinds were to be ' written in an ordinary, usual, and legible hand and character ', which turns out, on examination of surviving records, to be a mixture of secretary and italic. The restoration of Charles II brought back all the court hands of his father's day, displaying an exuberance and extravagance in no way reduced by their ten years' prohibition ; but the Act of 1731[3] achieved permanent success for the earlier temporary reforms, directing that the court hands should be replaced in records by ' such a common legible hand and character as the Acts of Parliament are usually engrossed in '. When the Act came into force in 1733 the departmental set hands ceased to be written ; but for one single purpose, the enrolment of Acts of Parliament on the Parliament Rolls sent into Chancery by the Clerk of the Parliaments,[4] the old Chancery hand continued to be used, in steadily coarsening and debased form, for as long as the Parliament Rolls are in manuscript. When the Rolls

[1] See above, p. 52.   [2] See above, p. 22.   [3] See above, p. 23.
[4] To be distinguished from the original Acts, whose writing had been selected as a model.

began (in 1849) to be made up of separate Acts printed on vellum, the manuscript signification of the royal assent appeared for a further ten years in the old Chancery hand,
corrupted by now into virtual illegibility (Plate XXX).

The 'hand and character' in which the Acts of Parliament were engrossed in 1731
had been evolved in the course of the preceding fifty years from the engrossing secretary
hand, described above, with some borrowing from italic. With the same ancestry as the
round hand, it nevertheless presents a very different appearance, since its basis remains
the vertical engrossing secretary with none of the slope and few of the letter-forms of italic
(Plate XXIX). It did not win permanent or lasting use for most of the records specified
in the Act of 1731, but in the Chancery Patent Rolls and Close Rolls it was written in a
form that varies remarkably little, from 1733 until the death of Queen Victoria (Plate XXXI).

I (a) Latin Bible, c. 850

I (b) Lindisfarne Gospels, c. 700 (glossed 10th cent.)

I (c) Domesday Book, 1086

II (a)   Royal Charter, 1110

II (b)   Private Charter, 1147

III (a) Monastic Deed, 1164

III (b) Monastic Deed, c. 1195

Private Charter of Confirmation, 1166–1202

IV (a)

Note of Fine, 1200

IV (b)

V (a)

Creation of a Chantry, 1229–30

V (b)

Private Charter of Confirmation, early 13th cent.

VI (a)

Letter to the Bishop of Chichester, 1222–44

VI (b)

Grant for Life, in Anglo-Norman French, 1291

Pleas at Durham, 1305

VII (a)

Dunelm̄. ¶ Riĉus de Hotoñ Prior Dunelm̄ quer̄
de Antonio Ep̄o Dunelm̄ q̄d cum idem
prior die Dñica p̄xima post festū Sc̄i Martini
anno dñi ⅺ r̄ nūc vicesimo apud Dunelm̄ accomodavit dc̄o Ep̄o duo paria Decretoᷓ unū par De-
cretaliū quemd librū qui vocat̄ Triptita Historia quamd librū qui vocat̄
Historia Angloᷓ unū Missale t unū librū qui

vocat̄ Liber Sc̄i Cuthb̄ti in quo secreta domus
scribunt̄ p̄c̄ ducentaᷓ libraᷓ retradend̄ sibi aut
successorib; suis ad volūtatē suā dc̄usq; Ep̄s sepius
p ip̄m priorē requisit̄ de dc̄is libr̄ restituend̄ hoc
face noluit immo illos detinuit t adhuc detinet
ad dampnū ip̄ius prior̄ t ecclie sue t̄c̄ viginti
libr̄. Et inde pduc̄ sectam t̄c̄.

VII (b)

The same passage in record type

Pleas at Beverley, 1308

VII (c)

VIII   Royal Letters Patent, 1317

IX (a)   Foot of fo. 96r of the Cartulary of St. Augustine's, Canterbury,
14th cent.

IX (b)   Top of fo. 96v of the same volume

Royal Letters Patent, 1348

X (a)

Proceedings in the King's Bench, 1383

X (b)

Proceedings in the Common Pleas, 1386

XI (a)

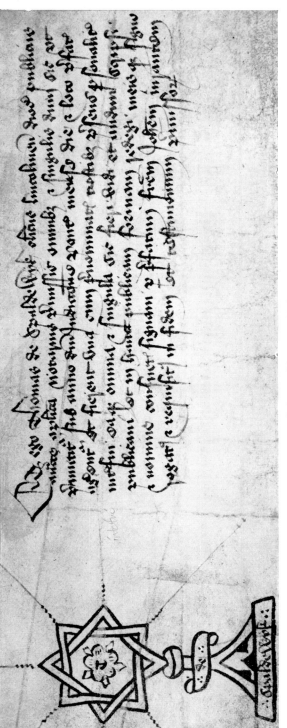

Notarial Certificate, 1396

XI (b)

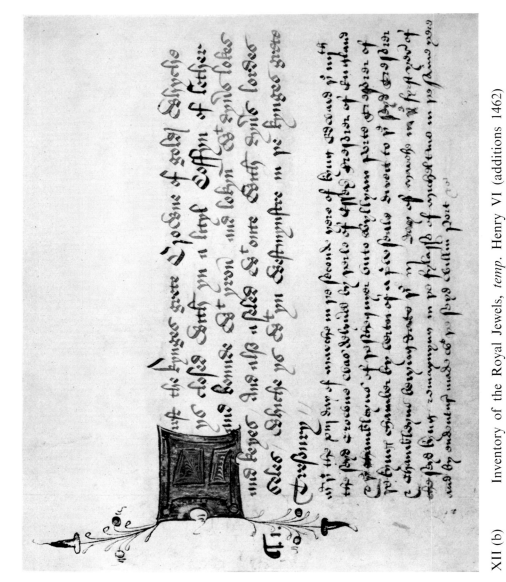

XII (a) Recipe for Ink, 15th cent.

XII (b) Inventory of the Royal Jewels, *temp.* Henry VI (additions 1462)

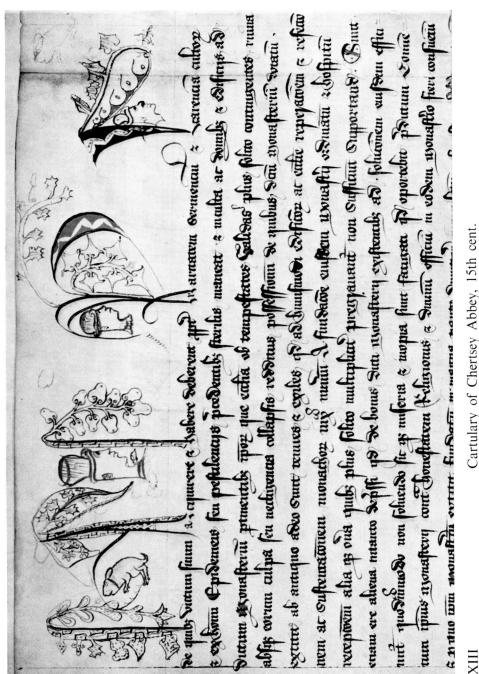

XIII

Cartulary of Chertsey Abbey, 15th cent.

Remission of Court, 1480

XIV (a)

Private Correspondence, 1480

XIV (b)

Signification of Excommunication, 1493

XV (a)

Foot of Fine, 1508

XV (b)

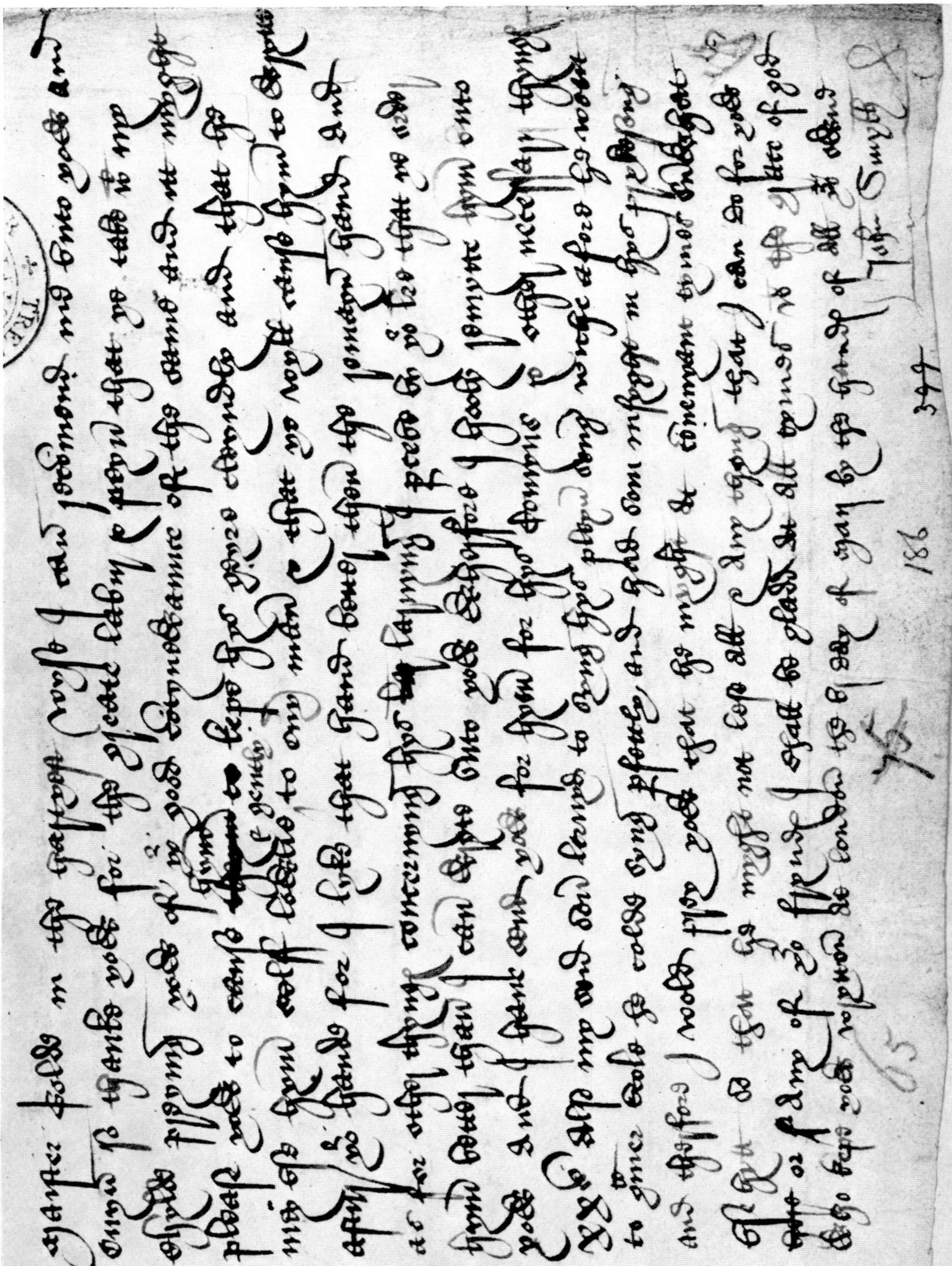

XVI Letter to a Cambridge Don, 1525

XVII (a) Letter written in English by Henry Gold (d. 1534)

XVII (b) Sermon notes in Latin by the same writer

XVIII   Enrolled Chancery Decree, 1562

XIX (a) Return of Commissioners administering the Oath of Supremacy, 1579

XIX (b) Letter to the Council, 1586

XX (a) Letter to Lord Burghley, 1589

XX (b) Chancery (Crown Office) Precedent Book, *c.* 1610

XXI (a)   Pipe Roll, 1628

Upon consideracon taken this day of the small
Letter written somly in entring the Pleadings in
the Courts at the Comon Law, and of the
Secretary hand in the English Courts mixed
with the Italian hand, wch is conceived will in
short tyme weare and become illegible
that it bee Certified by the Comrs in some fitt
place upon their next Certificates of the Abuses
of those Courts, to his Matts that as deserving
reformacon.

XXI (b)   Minute Book of Commissioners to inquire into Court Fees, 1635

XXII   Lord Treasurer's Remembrancer's Memoranda Roll, 1633

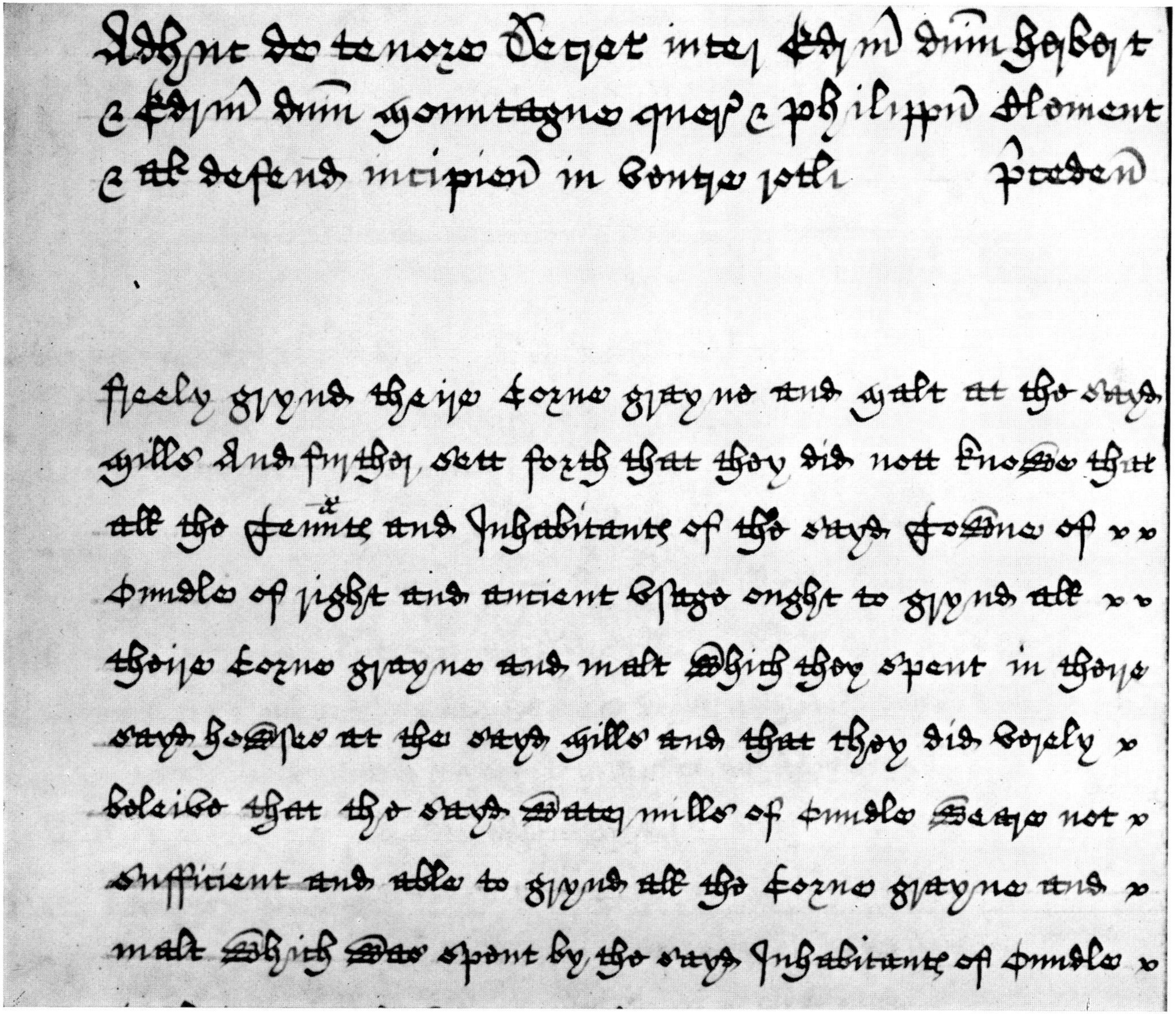

XXIII King's Remembrancer's Memoranda Roll, 1642

To the right hono.ble the Lords & others of
his Ma:ts most hono.ble Privy Councell.

The humble petition of Richard Beaumont
Apprentice unto James James an Apothecary, London

Humbly sheweth.

That yo.r pet.r was sent for by warr.t from the right hono: Sr ffrancis
Windebanke kt principall Secretary of State, and thereupon was
examyned by his hono.r for speaking some unadvised wordes, w.ch hee
did not deny; And upon report to yo.r Lopps of yo.r pet.rs humble
Confession, hee was iustly Committed by yo.r hono.rs to the prison of
the ffleete.

Your: Pet.r most humbly beseecheth yo.r Lopps in
regard that hee is heartily sorry that ever hee spake
such wordes, and doth purpose never to offend in the
like kinde that yo.r Lops out of yo.r accustomed
clemency wilbee pleased to give Order for his
Enlargement. And yo.r pet.r will pray &c.

At the Court at Whitehall the 28th of May 1640

Mr Secretary Windebanke. is prayed. to consider.
of this Pet.on and to take such Order therein, as —
with the advise of Mr Attorney Generall hee shall —
thinck good.

Edw: Nicholas

XXIV   Petition to the Privy Council, 1640

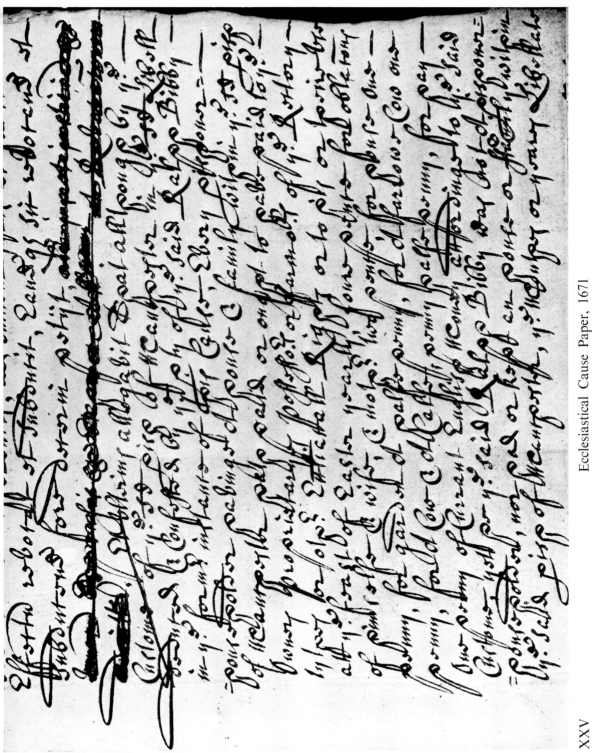

Ecclesiastical Cause Paper, 1671

XXV

XXVI

Recovery Roll, 1682

person being present shee was Unfortinately found guilty of Murther according
to the Severity of the Lawe of this Kingdome, and is adiudged to be Executed in
the City of Oxford on Thirsday next.

Now inasmuch as yo[ur] Peticon[er] is greatly sorrowfull for her sin, and much
more for the losse of her child and not fitt to dye being distracted in Mind.

Therefore yo[ur] poore Peticon[er] humbly implores yo[ur] Ma[jes]ties
Mercy in yo[ur] Princall Pardon and yo[ur] gratious Reprevio
from Execucion untill the said Pardon will issue forth.

And yo[ur] Peticon[er] as in duty bound shall pray &c.

Petition for Reprieve, 1682

XXVII

Coroner's Inquisition, 1729

XXIX   Proceedings in the King's Bench, Hilary-Easter, 1733

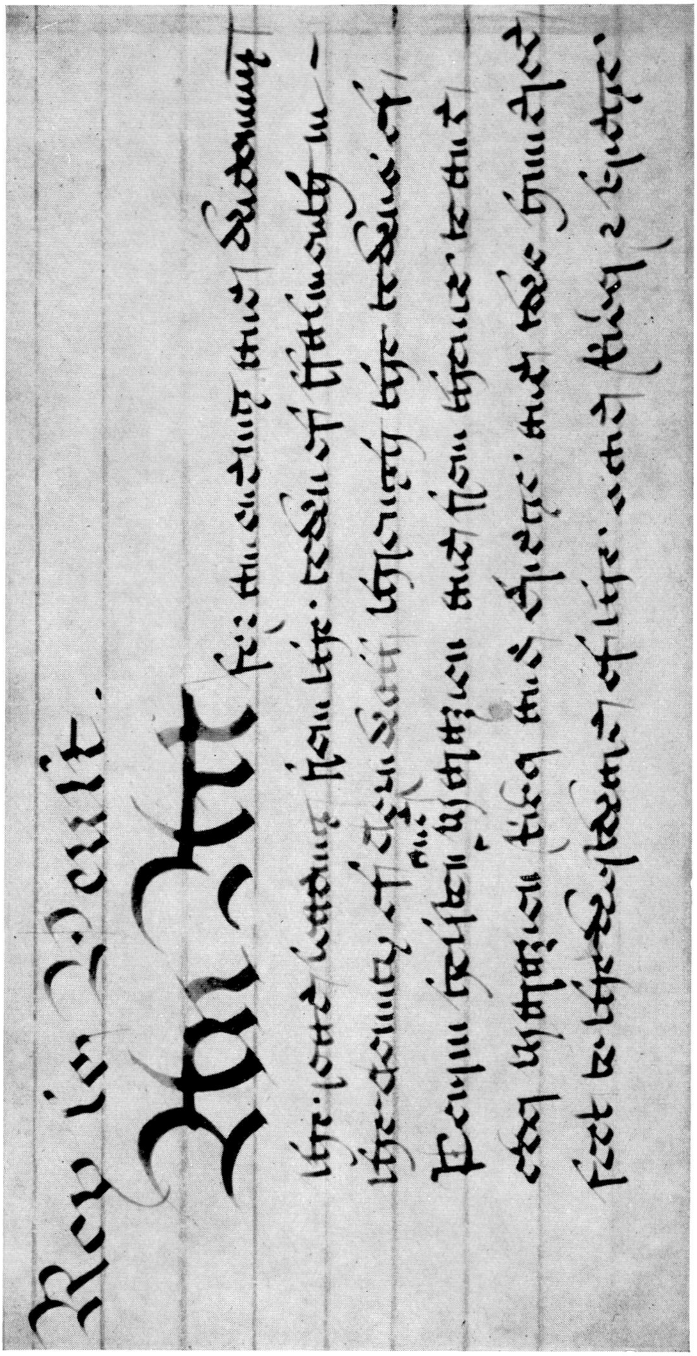

XXX (a) Parliament Roll, 1760

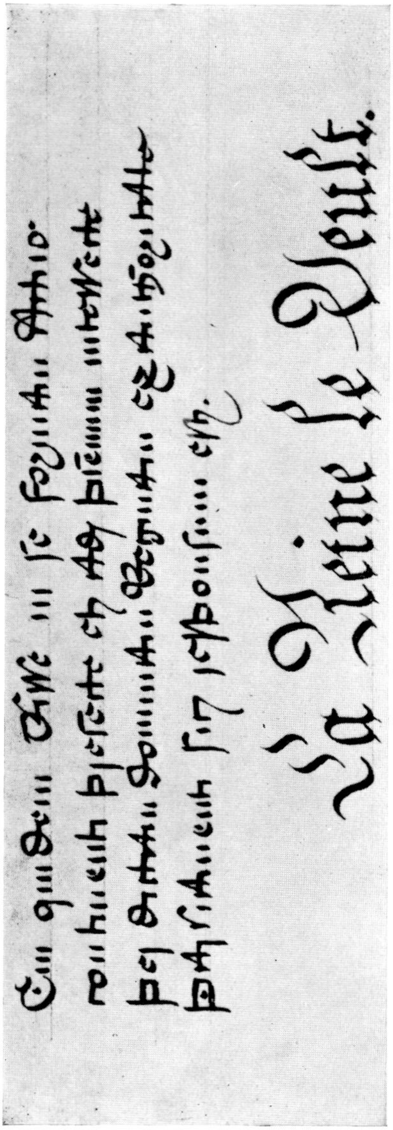

XXX (b) Parliament Roll, 1859

...pel or Building and the Land or Ground thereunto and belonging situate lying and being in the Town of Llanelly in the County of Carmarthen containing in the whole by common estimation forty two square yards or thereabouts be the same more or less which said premises are more particularly delineated and described in the ground plan thereof drawn in the margin of these presents Together with all ways and paths passages lights and easements waters water-courses privileges profits commodities advantages and appurts.. to the said hereditaments and premises belonging or in

have and to hold

XXXI   Deed Enrolled in Chancery, 1830

ARE ALL UNEEDING, AND ALMOST UNCONSCIOUS, GOOD SENSE,
AND A FIRM DESIRE TO ACT RIGHT ON ALL OCCASIONS,
TO THE BEST OF HER JUDGMENT;
WERE HER MOST DISTINGUISHING CHARACTERISTICS.
ACTIVITY OF MIND AND BODY,
SOUND HEALTH,
CHEERFUL MANNERS,
THE OPEN CONFIDENCE OF AN HONEST MIND,
THE LIVELY SERENITY OF AN EASY CONSCIENCE,
WITH A BENEVOLENT DISPOSITION,
AND HEREDITARY PERSONAL GRACES, BOTH OF FORM AND FACE,
WHICH EVEN IN AGE HAD NOT DISAPPEARED,
COMPLETE HER PICTURE.

BUT THAT HER GENTLE AND PURE MIND HAD MET
KIND, HARDSOME, HONEST, THE CHEERFUL, AND DISCREET,
AS DAUGHTER, WIFE, AND MOTHER, JUSTIFIED,
BY ALL WHO KNEW HER, KNEW AND REMEMBERED,
AND SPENT HER LIFE IN MAKING OTHERS BLEST—THEIR FRIEND WAS—
AND OTHER FRIEND IN SORROW TO HER
SURE DUTIES IN HER CHARACTER TO HER—
SHE YIELD WITH CALM AND CHEERFUL HEART,
WITH BEST AFFECTIONS—TOOK THE HUMBLEST PART;
AND SHEWETH—HER REMEMBRANCE OF THE HEART.

BURIED AT SNAITH IN THIS COUNTY.   The Hon.ble Marmaduke (Burton Dawnay) Langley (third Son) placed this Tablet 1836. ætat. LX.

XXXII   Monumental Inscription of Lora, Viscountess Downe, in York Minster

TRANSCRIPTS OF THE PASSAGES
REPRODUCED IN THE PLATES

Preliminary Note

With three exceptions (whose custody is indicated in the headings to the relevant transcripts) the documents illustrated in the plates and transcribed in the succeeding pages are all in the Public Record Office. In the transcript-headings these documents have been cited by their official class-numbers (to which a key is provided below) and sub-numbers.

Chancery

C.47	*Miscellanea*
C.54	*Close Rolls*
C.65	*Parliament Rolls*
C.78	*Decree Rolls*
C.85	*Significations of Excommunication*
C.193	*Crown Office Miscellaneous Books*
C.202H	*Cancelled Engrossments, etc., of Letters Patent*

Common Pleas

C.P.25(1)	*Feet of Fines, Series I*
C.P.40	*Plea Rolls*
C.P.43	*Recovery Rolls*

Duchy of Lancaster

D.L.36	*Cartae Miscellaneae*

Exchequer, Treasury of the Receipt

E.31	*Domesday Book*
E.36	*Books*
E.40	*Ancient Deeds, Series A*

Exchequer, King's (Queen's) Remembrancer

E.159	*Memoranda Rolls*
E.164	*Miscellaneous Books, Series I*

Exchequer, Augmentation Office

E.315	*Miscellaneous Books*

Exchequer, Lord Treasurer's Remembrancer

E.368	*Memoranda Rolls*
E.372	*Pipe Rolls*

Justices Itinerant

J.I.1	*Assize Rolls, etc.*

Queen's Bench, Crown Side

Q.B.11	*Indictments, Modern (Out-Counties)*
Q.B.26	*Curia Regis Rolls*
Q.B.27	*Coram Rege Rolls*
Q.B.28	*Crown Rolls*

Special Collections

S.C.1	*Ancient Correspondence*
S.C.2	*Court Rolls*

State Paper Office

S.P.1	*State Papers Domestic, Henry VIII*
S.P.12	*State Papers Domestic, Elizabeth I*
S.P.16	*State Papers Domestic, Charles I*
S.P.29	*State Papers Domestic, Charles II*

There is no universally approved way of printing the texts of manuscript archives. In most of the matters covered by the numbered paragraphs which follow practice varies widely and there is no evidence to suggest that editors are willing to purchase the benefits of uniformity at the cost of any of their own preferences. When a committee of experienced scholars was invited about thirty-five years ago to 'suggest principles upon which historical documents should be edited', its members were careful to disavow in their report any implied obligation on themselves to practise individually what they collectively preached.[1]   Perhaps there could be no more tactful intimation that we are here in the realm not of easily demonstrable right and wrong but of predilection and personal taste. Since these are notoriously unsuitable subjects for disputation, no anticipatory defence is offered here for the following principles adopted in printing these transcripts.

1. (a) Abbreviations whose meaning seemed to be beyond doubt have been extended and the expanded forms used which agreed with the writers' observable practice.
   (b) Abbreviation-marks of uncertain significance have been represented by apostrophes.
   (c) In documents in English those abbreviation-marks which appeared to be otiose have been ignored in transcription.
2. (a) The spellings of the manuscripts have been retained, but *i, j, u,* and *v* have been rendered by *j, i, v,* and *u* respectively wherever modern usage required the change. The form printed for the capital of *f* is *F* (never *ff*).
   (b) The digraphs *æ* and *œ* and the ' tagged ' *e* have been printed as *ae* and *oe*, except in the transcript of Plate I (b), where Anglo-Saxon *æ* is preserved.   The runes (barred *d*, *thorn* and *wen*), Middle-English *yogh*, and *y* replacing *th*, have all been kept.
3. No attempt has been made to reproduce the punctuation of the manuscripts or to adhere to their use of capitals.
4. Matter drawn from the immediate contexts of the passages reproduced, or offered conjecturally to supply accidental omissions and losses from the original manuscripts, has been printed between square brackets.

[1] Institute of Historical Research *Bulletin*, Vol. I (1923), p. 6 : ' It [the Report on Editing Historical Documents] is the work of the committee as a whole, but does not bind any individual member to any particular statement.'

Plate I (a)   Latin Bible   *c.* 850
(British Museum, Add. MS. 10546)

Carolingian minuscules, with displayed matter in square capitals (l. 10), rustic capitals (ll. 3 and 9) and uncials (l. 4).   Written at Tours.

[I John v. 20 to II John 1]

[. . . et dedit nobis sensum ut cognoscamus Deum verum et si]mus in vero filio ejus.   Hic est verus Deus et vita aeterna.   Filioli, custodite vos a simulacris.

EXPLICIT EPISTOLA SANCTI JOHANNIS PRIMA

INCIPIUNT CAPITULA EPISTOLAE SECUNDAE

[I] De diligendis cultoribus veritatis.
[II] De dilectione alterna quod non sit novum ac rude praeceptum.
[III] De seductoribus qui in mundo abundant.
[IIII] De non dicendo *Have* his aliud qui praeferunt dogma.
[V] De sua praesentia in qua narrandum omnia reservavit.   EXPLICIUNT.

INCIPIT EJUSDEM SECUNDA

[S]enior electae dominae et natis ejus quos ego diligo in veritate ; et non ego solus sed et om[nes qui cognoverunt veritatem . . .]

Plate I (b)   Lindisfarne Gospels   *c.* 700 (glossed 10th cent.)
(British Museum, Cotton MS. Nero D. iv)

Insular half-uncials, glossed in insular minuscules

[St. Luke ii. 13–15]

Et subito facta est cum angelo multitudo militiae caelestis laudantium Deum et dicentium, Gloria in altissimis Deo, et in terra pax hominibus bonae voluntatis.   Factum est ut discesserunt ab eis angeli in caelum.

Anglo-Saxon[1] :

And sona aporden þæs mið engle menigo hiorodes heofonlic hergendra God and cuo-eðendra puldor in heannisum Gode and in eordo sib monnum godes pillo.   Aporden is þæte fearradon from him ða englas in heofne.

[1] Although the Anglo-Saxon is for convenience here printed separately from the Latin, it is, of course, not a formal translation but a word-by-word gloss.

Plate I (c)   Domesday Book   1086
(E. 31/2, fo. 142r)

Formal book or business hand

IN HERFORD HUNDREDO

In Wermelai tenet Aluuinus Dodesone ii. hidas et dimidiam de rege.   Terra est ii. carucis, et ibi sunt, cum vi. villanis et uno servo.   Pratum ii. carucis.   Pastura ad pecuniam.   Silva cl. porcis.   Inter totum valet xl. solidos ; quando recepit, l. solidos ; tempore regis Eduuardi, lx. solidos.   Hoc manerium tenuit Wluuardus homo Asgari Stalri, et vendere potuit.   Hoc manerium fuit venditum iii. markis auri post adventum regis Willelmi.

Petrus quidam burgensis tenet ii. hidas de rege in Dodesdone.

Plate II (a)   Royal Charter   1110
(E. 40/14406)

Formal business hand

Henricus rex Anglorum Roberto episcopo Lincolniensi et Gisleberto vicecomiti et omnibus baronibus et omnibus fidelibus suis Francis et Anglis et omnibus mercatoribus totius Angliae salutem.   Sciatis me concessisse Sancto Benedicto de Ramesia et Sancto Ivoni de Selepe feriam a die Mercurii in Pascha usque ad octavum diem ita bene et honorifice cum soca et saca et toll et tiem et infangeneteof et cum omnibus consuetudinibus sicut aliqua feria melius habet in tota Anglia.   Et volo et praecipio ut omnes ad eam venientes et in ea existentes et inde redeuntes firmam pacem meam habeant.   Testibus Roberto episcopo Lincolniensi et Roberto comite de Mellent et Hamone Dapifero et Gisleberto vicecomite et Willelmo de Hoctona.   Apud Brantonam in anno quo rex dedit filiam suam imperatori.

Plate II (b)   Private Charter   1147
                               (D.L. 36/1/214)

Business hand

Hugo Tyrellus omnibus hominibus suis et amicis salutem.   Sciatis me dedisse et concessisse
manerium meum de Lahingeham et omnia manerii pertinentia Gervasio de Corhella
finabiliter in feudo et hereditate ipsi et heredibus suis de me et de meis heredibus tenenda,
reddendo michi per annum ipse vel heredes sui michi vel meis heredibus pro omnibus
servitiis unam cuppam argenti de pondere trium marcarum Londoniensium, cuicumque
illam jubebo reddendam vel heredes mei Gervasio predicto vel heredibus suis, scilicet infra
octo dies Pasche, et hoc sine omni alia causa vel forisfactura, etiam si terminus Pasche
transisset, nisi de sola cuppa reddenda.   Et si ego vel heredes mei eundem Gervasium
vel heredes suos incausare vel inplacitare voluerimus, Londoniis placitum illud teneatur.
Et pro hac donatione et concessione et conventione concedenda dedit michi Gervasius
idem c. marcas argenti ad iter meum dirigendum in Iherussalem.   Testibus istis, Ricardus[1]
de Luci Hengelram de Albemarla Bernierus de Claro Monte Wido de Mustrol Rogerus
de Fraxino.   Et de hoc feudo factus est meus homo.[2]

> [1] The names of the witnesses are erroneously in the nominative.
> [2] The last eight words are a later addition.

Plate III (a)   Monastic Deed   1164
                               (E. 315/53/213)

Formal book or business hand

J U S T U S   D O M I N U S   E T   J U S T I C I A S[1]

Sciant filii sancte[2] matris ecclesiae[3] tam pr(a)esentes quam futuri quod ego Rogerus abbas
Rading' et conventus pro anima gloriosi regis Henrici[4] primi et pia peticione[5] domini nostri
regis Henrici secundi concessimus canonicis de Brumora ecclesiam de Wichebiria tenendam
de nobis pro v. libris incensi annuatim ecclesiae[6] nostre[7] persolvendis ad Pascha ; sed et
omnes priores de Brumora sibi invicem succedentes pro hac concessione in perpetuum
conservanda sicut clerici nostri facient nobis fidelitatem in capitulo nostro.   Actum est
hoc anno m°. c°. lx°. iiii°. Incarnationis Dominicae[3] quando dedicata fuit ecclesia Rading'
in pr(a)esentia regis Henrici et Thome[8] archiepiscopi Cantuarie[9] et Henrici episcopi
Wintonie[8] et aliorum plurimorum episcoporum comitum baronum et multitudinis populorum.

> [1] The lower halves of these words (taken from Ps. xi. 7, *Quoniam justus Dominus et justicias dilexit*)
> are visible in the upper margin.   When documents were executed in duplicate, both texts were written on
> the same piece of parchment, which was then divided into two by a cut passing through a word or words
> in capitals occupying the space between them.   The usual choice for this space was one of the many
> alternative spellings of the word *chirographum* (cf. Plate III (b)), but other words, alphabets, and Scriptural
> tags, as here, are not uncommon.   In later practice the dividing cut was serrated or indented : hence the
> term ' indenture '.
> [2] *e* not tagged.   [3] *e* tagged.   [4] *secundi* struck through.
> [5] In *ll*. 8 and 9 palatalised *t* has not been replaced by *c*.
> [6] *e* tagged.   [7] Interlined. *e* not tagged.
> [8] *e* not tagged.   [9] Spelling deduced from *Wintonie* in the next line.

Plate III (b)   Monastic Deed   c. 1195
                                (E. 40/14188)

Semi-cursive business hand

C I R O G R A F U M[1]

Sciant presentes et futuri quod ego Willelmus prior de Sancto Pancracio et conventus concedimus et hac presenti carta confirmamus canonicis Sancte Crucis de Heringeham ecclesiam de Heringeham cum omnibus pertinenciis suis et terram de la Helle quam Willelmus[2] tenet,[3] habendam et tenendam de nobis in perpetuum pro octo solidis annuatim nobis reddendis ad duos terminos, scilicet ad festum Sancti Michaelis iiii. solidis et ad Pascha iiii. solidis ; et predictus[4] Willelmus[5] tenebit[6] de ipsis quamdiu vixerit,[7] reddendo eis eandem pensionem quam nobis persolvebat.[8] Hec concessio firma et stabilis, quamdiu predicti canonici solvendo fideles extiterint, erit.

> [1] The lower half of this (abbreviated) word appears in the upper margin. See note 1 to Plate III (a)·
> [2] *et Thomas* struck through.   [3] Altered by expunction from *tenent*.
> [4] Altered by obliteration from *predicti*.   [5] *et Thomas* struck through.
> [6] Altered by expunction from *tenebunt*. The single subscript dot deletes one of the minims of *u* and, presumably, the *n* implied in the mark of abbreviation above it.
> [7] Altered by expunction from *vixerint*.
> [8] Altered by an ingenious use of obliteration from *persolverunt*, the *b* being superimposed on *r* and the *a* contrived from *u* with the tittle, representing *n*, above it.

Plate IV (a)   Private Charter of Confirmation   1166–1202
                                (E. 315/36/131)

Formal book or business hand

Sciant qui sunt et qui futuri sunt quod ego Stephanus de Cursun concessi et presenti carta confirmavi Deo et Sancte Marie et monachis de Brueria unam hidam terre et viginti acras de feudo meo in Sibbefordia quas Willelmus de Sibbeford eis dedit et carta sua confirmavit ; et confirmo eis quantum infra clausuras eorum continetur et totam terram quam ruperunt et coluerunt de pastura ejusdem ville et nominatim juxta Tuamwellam quantum pertinet ad croftam unius hide, et preterea unam virgatam terre de dominio ejusdem Sibbeford cum pratis et pascuis et omnibus aisiamentis ad eam pertinentibus. Cujus virgate acre[1] sic asignate sunt, nominatim in Westfeldo quatuor acras [*sic*] in Bromhulle et octo in Wudeweia vertentes et tres ad Wudeuuellam in Nordfeldo sex acras [*sic*] in Berhfur[lung . . .]

> [1] The preceding two words are written in inverted order and marked for transposition. See above, p. 48.

Plate IV (b)   Note of Fine   1200
                                (Q.B. 26/16, m. 4)

Cursive court or business hand

Hec est finalis concordia facta in curia domini regis inter Robertum de Mara petentem et Jordanum de Mara tenentem de feodo j. militis cum pertinentiis in Kedestorhne et in

Cernai, scilicet quod predictus Robertus quietum clamavit prenominato Jordano totum jus et totum clamium quod habuit vel habere clamavit in prenominato feodo militis in Kedestorhne et in Cernai. Et pro hac quieta clamantia dedit predictus Jordanus prenominato Roberto c. solidos et preterea dabit idem Jordanus prenominato Roberto dimidiam marcam argenti ad se vestiendum per annum, scilicet ad festum Sancti Michaelis quamdiu idem Robertus vixerit quousque idem Jordanus[1] assignaverit ipsi Roberto[1] in certo eccl[es]iastico beneficio c. solidatas redditus.

[1] Over an erasure.

Plate V (a)   Creation of a Chantry   1229–30
                                (D.L. 36/1/247)

Semi-cursive court or business hand

Omnibus Christi fidelibus hoc scriptum visuris Ricardus Dei gratia abbas et conventus de Walth' salutem in Domino. Noveritis nos caritative concessisse domino Hugoni de Nevile quod intra septa curie nostre duos capellanos sustinebimus sumptibus nostris in perpetuum ; quorum unus perpetuo celebrabit divina pro dicto domino Hugone post obitum suum et pro anima domine Johanne uxoris sue et heredum suorum et pro animabus omnium abbatum et fratrum nostrorum et omnium benefactorum ecclesie nostre ; alius vero capellanus perpetuo celebrabit de Sancto Spiritu vel de Domina vel de festo in magnis sollempnitatibus pro prefato domino Hugone et Johanne herede suo et omnibus successoribus suis et pro omnibus benefactoribus nostris. Preterea concessimus predictis domino H. et Johanni heredi suo quod post obitum eorum fient pro eis a quolibet canonico sacerdote[1] inter nos unum tricennale missarum et a quolibet alio inferioris ordinis decem psalteria et tricennale missarum quod dicitur tricennale Sancti Gregorii et perpetuum annuale missarum sicut fit pro canonicis nostris defunctis et in eorum obitu sollempne servicium[2] in conventu ; et nomina eorum in martirologio scribentur eorumque anniversarium singulis annis perpetuo celebrabitur. Et preter hec specialem participationem eis et omnibus successoribus suis concessimus omnium spiritualium bonorum que fient in ecclesia nostra in perpetuum. Et ne possit de hac nostra concessione ab aliquo dubitari hoc scriptum communis sigilli nostri appositione confirmavimus.

[1] The preceding two words are written in inverted order and marked for transposition. See p. 48.
[2] Elsewhere (in the penultimate and last lines of the manuscript) palatalised *t* has not been replaced by *c*.

Plate V (b)   Private Charter of Confirmation   Early 13th cent.
                                (E. 315/43/6)

' Gothic ' book hand

Omnibus ad quos presentis scripti noticia pervenerit Willelmus de Kingesford' salutem. Noverit universitas vestra me concessisse et presenti carta mea confirmasse monachis de Bruer' unam hidam terre in Sesnecot' de feudo meo cum omnibus pertinentiis suis et libertatibus, illam videlicet hydam quam Willelmus filius Willelmi de Pundeveske eisdem monachis dedit et carta sua confirmavit ; tenendam bene et in pace sicut carta mea quam dedi Willelmo patri prefati Willelmi de eadem terra testatur. Et ut hec mea concessio firma et stabilis inperpetuum permaneat presenti scripto sigillo meo munito eam confirmavi. Et pro hac confirmatione prefati monachi dederunt michi tres marcas argenti. Hiis testibus, Willelmo de Estun' Henrico de Cheurigwrth' Roberto de Slouthre Simone de Swelle Hugone de Cundicot' Waltero de Campeden' Ricardo de Tiwe et multis aliis.

Plate VI (a)   Letter to the Bishop of Chichester   1222–44
                                        (S.C. 1/6/64)

Cursive court or business hand

Hactenus clementissimo semper autem reverendo domino suo R. Dei gratia Cicestrensi episcopo suus in omnibus devotus clericus magister W. de Leuekenor' salutem[1] in eo qui salus est omnium. Auditis nuper verbis vestris duris et asperis concussum est dolore vehementi cor meum, erubuit facies mea, et conturbata sunt omnia ossa mea.[2] Putabam utique, immo confidebam in Domino, invenisse vos benignos [et] affabiles more solito, et ecce mutata sunt omnia, ita quod gemens et dolens cum Job dico, ' Mutatus es michi in crudelem.' [3] Set hec est unica consolatio mea, quod vos more pii patris qui filium dilectum flagellat quem recipit,[4] quem vero odio habet necgligit castigare, sic forsitan et vos, de quibus concipio fiduciam quam de Domino legitur : ' Cum iratus fueris misericordie recordaberis.' [5] In hoc autem quod me arguitis, quod post liberam vestram vocationem juxta ecclesie vestre consuetudinem non resedi, forsitan memorie vestre non oc[cur]rit quod per iiij[or]. annos postquam ad partem sollicitudinis vestre vocatus essem laboravi legendo [et] predicando plus quam qui presesserunt me, nec usquam recessi sine speciali et urgenti necessitate propria vel communi. Quod autem anno preterito recessi ab Anglia, coegit votum peregrinandi diuturnum ; et quod per tantum temporis moram feci, compulit me corporis mei multiplex infirmitas. Reversus quidem nunc, in ecclesia vestra stare propono, legendo ut prius et laborando : prius utique fatigati erunt auditores audiendo quam ego legendo. Si autem linguis veneficis et invidis malum de me vobis suadentibus ad gratiam vestram pristinam et pristinam familiaritatem me redire non permittitis, paratus ero dimissis omnibus sequi Deum et ad statum vite scolastice redire cum gaudio potius quam in ecclesia vestra affligi dolore. Nunc igitur, si vestro animo sederit ut legam hoc anno instanti, accomodetis michi librum Exodi, et mittatis michi per latorem presentium. Valete.

[1] Interlined.   [2] Cf. Vulgate, Ps. vi. 3 and xxx. 11.
[3] Job xxx. 21.   [4] Hebr. xii. 6.   [5] Hab. iii. 2.

Plate VI (b)   Grant for Life   1291
                                        (D.L. 36/1/108)

Cursive court or business hand

S C R I P T U M[1]

Henri de Lascy conte de Nichole e conestable de Cestre seingnur de Ross e de Reweynok' a tuz ceus ke cest escrit verront ou orront saluz en nostre seingnur. Sachez nus aver done e graunte par cest nostre present escrit a Johan le Chapman nostre warenner de Hengstrigg' tote la terre e le tenement ke Willame le Warenner jadis tint de nus en nostre maner de Kingeston' en Dorsete ; a aver e a tenir de nus e de nos heirs e de nos asingnez au dit Johan a tote sa vie ; rendaunt ent par an a nus e a nos heirs ou a nos assingnez vint souz desterlings, cest asaveir a la Purificacion de Nostre Dame a la Nativite de Seint Johan le Baptistre e a la Seint Michel par owel porcions pur tote manere de servises a nus e a nos heirs apendaunz ; e nus Henri de Lascy e nos heirs tote la devauntdite terre e tenement au dit Johan a tote [s]a vie en la fourme avauntdite garantiroms. En tesmoine de queu chose a cest [escrit endente a la partie demoraunt vers Johan avoms' fet mettre nostre seel . . .].

¹ The lower halves of these letters are visible along the indented upper edge of the document. See note 1 to Plate III (a) above.

Plate VII (a)   Pleas at Durham   1305
                                 (J.I. 1/228, m. 5)

Cursive court or business hand

[*Dunelm'*.] Ricardus de Hoton' prior Dunelm' queritur de Antonio episcopo Dunelmensi quod cum idem prior die Dominica proxima post festum Sancti Martini anno domini regis nunc vicesimo apud Dunelm' accomodavit dicto episcopo duo paria Decretorum, unum par Decretalium, quemdam¹ librum qui vocatur Tripartita Historia, quamdam Bibliam, quemdam librum qui vocatur Historia Anglorum, unum missale et unum librum qui vocatur Liber Sancti Cuthberti, in quo secreta domus scribuntur, precii ducentarum librarum, retradenda sibi aut successoribus suis ad voluntatem suam, dictusque episcopus sepius per ipsum priorem requisitus de dictis libris restituendis² hoc facere noluit, immo illos detinuit et adhuc detinet, ad dampnum ipsius prioris et ecclesie sue etc. viginti librarum ; et inde producit sectam etc.

¹ There is one minim too many in this word in the manuscript.
² Substituted for original *restaurandis*.

Plate VII (b)

This is the record-type version of the passage illustrated in Plate VII (a). It is reproduced from Sir Thomas Hardy's *Registrum Palatinum Dunelmense*, Vol. IV (1878), pp. 43–4.

Plate VII (c)   Pleas at Beverley   1308
                                (S.C. 2/211/12, m. 4)

Cursive court or business hand

Nicholaus le Barbour summonitus fuit ad respondendum Johanni de Marton' de placito convencionis, et unde idem Johannes queritur quod die Mercurii proxima post festum Sancte Margarete Virginis anno regni regis nunc primo idem Nicholaus manucepit ad sanandum unam plagam in tibio¹ ejusdem Johannis pro duobus solidis, de quibus solvit ei xij. denarios, et xij. denarios solvisse debuit quando sanatus² fuerit ; et dictus Nicholaus infra terciam diem proximo sequentem in partes Holderness' se elongavit, propter quod idem Johannes ivit ad Beverlacum ad quendam Robertum Medicum et tradidit ei iiij. solidos pro predicta plaga sananda. Hec sibi fecit contra convencionem etc., unde deterioratus est et dampnum habet ad valenciam[3] dimidie marce etc.; et inde producit sectam. Et dictus Nicholaus venit et defendit vim[4] etc. quando etc.; et bene recognoscit convencionem etc., set dicit quod tradidit eidem [Johanni medicinam ad plagam suam sanandam dum ipse infra partes Holdern' moram traxisset . . .]

[1] Recte *tibia*.   [2] Amended to (or from?) *sanata* (*sc.* plaga).
[3] The manuscript inserts a superfluous *et* here.   [4] Obliterating *etc.*

Plate VIII   Royal Letters Patent   1317
                              (C. 202 H 7/7)

Ceremonious court or business hand

Edwardus Dei gracia rex Anglie dominus Hibernie et dux Aquitannie omnibus ad quos presentes littere pervenerint salutem. Sciatis quod de gracia nostra speciali concessimus et licenciam dedimus pro nobis et heredibus nostris quantum in nobis est dilectis nobis in Christo . .[1] priori et conventui de Novo Loco in Shirewode quod ipsi terras tenementa et redditus ad valenciam viginti librarum annuarum juxta verum valorem eorundem tam de feodo suo proprio quam alieno, exceptis terris tenementis et redditibus que de nobis tenentur in capite, adquirere possint, tenenda sibi et successoribus suis imperpetuum, statuto de terris et tenementis ad manum mortuam non ponendis edito non obstante, dum tamen per inquisiciones inde modo debito faciendas et in cancellaria nostra vel heredum nostrorum rite retornandas compertum sit quod id fieri poterit absque prejudicio nostro aut alterius cujuscumque. In cujus rei testimonium has litteras nostras fieri fecimus patentes. Teste me ipso apud Notingham vicesimo quarto die Julii anno regni nostri undecimo.

                                        Per ipsum regem.   March'.

[1] *Gemipunctus.* See above, p. 46.

Plate IX (a and b)   Cartulary of St. Augustine's Canterbury   14th cent.
                       (E. 164/27, fo. 96r and 96v)

Non-calligraphic book hand

(a) (Bottom of fo. 96r)

[. . . rectas disposiciones . . . favore nos decet efficaci prosequi, pre]sertim ubi causa pietatis noscitur exerceri. Cum igitur ecclesia[m] vestri manerii de Chistelet usibus infirmancium congregacionis vestre, que multis expensis dicitur indigere, a longis retro temporibus duxeritis ascribendam, eamque bone memorie Theobaldus archiepiscopus Cantuariensis ad eosdem usus nobis[1] duxerit postmodum confirmandam, de consensu vestro nichilominus statuens ne fructus prefate ecclesie in alios[2] quam in usus predictos futuris temporibus convertantur, quod per bone memorie Ricardum ejusdem archiepiscopi successorem extitit confirmatum,

(b) (Top of fo. 96v)

de concensu vestro nichilominus statuens ne fructus prefate ecclesie in alios quam in usus predictos[3] nichilominus ab eodem archiepiscopo, sui capituli accedente concensu, eidem ecclesie immunitate concessa quod ab omnibus donis et procuracionibus suis et suorum officialium sit immunis, prout in ipsius archiepiscopi litteris inde confectis plenius continetur, nos justis vestris precibus grato concur[rentes assensu . . .]

　　　　[1] Recte *vobis*.　　　　　　　　　　[2] Corrected, by obliteration, from *alias*.
　　　　[3] The preceding fifteen words, which duplicate a passage already written on fo. 96r, are deleted by being enclosed between the first two and the last three letters of the word *vacat*.　See above, p. 48.

Plate X (a)　　　　　　　　Royal Letters Patent　　　　　　　　1348
　　　　　　　　　　　　　　(C. 202 H 15/4)

Ceremonious court or business hand

Edwardus Dei gracia rex Anglie et Francie et dominus Hibernie omnibus ad quos presentes littere pervenerint salutem.　Sciatis quod de gracia nostra speciali concessimus pro nobis et heredibus nostris dilecto et fideli nostro Hugoni de Monte Gomeri manerium de Lyndon' cum pertinenciis in comitatu Rotel' quod Johannes de Monte Gomeri miles defunctus nuper tenuit ad vitam suam ex concessione nostra ; habendum et tenendum eidem Hugoni ad totam vitam suam, reddendo inde nobis per annum ad scaccarium nostrum extentam inde factam ; ita quod post mortem ejusdem Hugonis manerium predictum cum pertinenciis ad nos et heredes nostros integre revertatur.　In cujus rei testimonium has litteras nostras fieri fecimus patentes.　Teste me ipso apud Westmonasterium primo die Aprilis anno regni nostri Anglie vicesimo secundo regni vero nostri Francie nono.

　　　　　　　　　　　　　　　　　　Per breve de privato sigillo.

Plate X (b)　　　　　　　Proceedings in the King's Bench　　　　　　1383
　　　　　　　　　　　　　　(Q.B. 27/490, Rex 3)

Cursive court or business hand

[*Cant'*.]　Jurata diversorum hundredorum comitatus predicti alias, scilicet termino Sancte Trinitatis anno regni regis nunc sexto, coram domino rege apud Cantebr' presentavit quod Willelmus Gore probator captus et in gaola domini regis castri Cantebr' detentus et laicus erat tempore capcionis corporis sui et jam per assensum et licenciam Johannis Darcy gaolarii et janitoris[1] ibidem irruditus est et informatus de leterura per Johannem vicarium ecclesie de le Roundechirche in villa de Cantebrigge per diversas vices, videlicet a festo Nativitatis Sancti Johannis Baptiste anno regni regis Ricardi secundi post Conquestum septimo usque in hodiernum diem—per quod preceptum [fuit] vicecomiti quod caperet prefatum Johannem vicarium ecclesie predicte si etc.—et modo, scilicet in octabis Sancti Michaelis isto eodem termino coram domino rege apud Westmonasterium [venit predictus Johannes . . .]

　　　　　　　[1] There is one minim too many in this word in the manuscript.

Plate XI (a)   Proceedings in the Common Pleas   1386
                              (C.P. 40/500, rot. 304*d*)

Common-law hand (primitive form), with additions in cursive

[. . . dicunt quod . . . Johannes de Maxstoke mortuus est . . . et proferunt . . . litteras testamentarias . . . per quas satis liquet curie hic ipsos fore] executores ejusdem Johannis et habere administracionem etc., et dicunt quod execucio debiti predicti adhuc restat facienda, et petunt quod ipsi ad prosecucionem ejusdem debiti admittantur modo et forma quibus idem Johannes de Maxstoke in vita sua prosequebatur etc. ; et admittuntur etc.   Ideo fiat eisdem executoribus breve inde per statutum etc. in forma qua prefatus Johannes de Maxstoke in vita sua prosequebatur etc. ; et qualiter etc. [vicecomes] scire faciat hic in octabis Sancte Trinitatis etc.   Ad[1] quem diem vicecomes non misit [breve]. Ideo sicut prius fiat inde breve per statutum etc. in forma predicta returnabile hic in octabis Sancti Hillarii etc.

[1] Change of hand.

Plate XI (b)   Notarial Certificate   1396
                              (C. 47/15/1/26)

Bastard hand

Et ego Thomas de Spaldewyk' clericus Lincolniensis diocesis publicus auctoritate apostolica notarius premissis omnibus et singulis dum sic ut premittitur sub anno Domini indiccione pontificatu mense die et loco prefatis agerentur et fierent una cum prenominatis testibus presens personaliter interfui eaque omnia et singula sic fieri vidi et audivi scripsi publicavi et in hanc publicam formam redegi meisque signo[1] et nomine consuetis signavi per prefatum fratrem Johannem jurantem rogatus et requisitus in fidem et testimonium premissorum.

[1] The notary's mark, a means of authentication, is the device (incorporating the name *T. de Spaldewyk'*) which appears on the left of the certificate.

Plate XII (a)   Recipe for Ink   15th cent.
                              (C. 47/34/1/3)

Bastard hand

To make hynke take galles and coporos[1] or vitrial (quod idem est) and gumme, of everyche a quartryn oþer helf quartryn, and a halfe quartryn of galles more ; and breke þe galles a ij. oþer a iij. and put ham togedere everyche on in a pot and stere hyt ofte ; and[2] wythinne ij. wykys after ȝe mow wryte þerwyþ.

   [3]Yf ȝe have a quartryn of everyche, take a quarte of watyr ; yf halfe a quartryn of everyche, þan take half a quarte of watyr.

     [1] *and* expunged.   [2] *wyȝt* struck through.   [3] *Yogh* struck through.

Plate XII (b)   Inventory of the Royal Jewels   *temp.* Henry VI,
                                 (E. 36/84, p. 29)   additions 1462

Bastard hand, additions in a ' splayed' hand

1. First the kynges grete crowne of gold, whyche ys closed withyn a lityl coffyn of lether
and bounde with yron and lokyn with dyvers lokes and keyes and also aseled withoute with
dyvers lordes seles ; whiche ys withyn Westmynstre in þe kynges grete tresoury.

Memorandum[1] þat the xiij. day of Marche in þe seconde yere of Kyng Edward þe
iiij[th] the seyd crowne was delyvered by þerle of Essex tresorer of England and þe chamberleyns of þeschequyer unto Wyllyam Porte tresorer of þe kynges chamber by vertu of a
prive seale direct to þe seyd tresorer and chamberleyns beryng date þe iij. day of Marche
in þe fyrst yere of the seyd kyng remaynyng in þe fylasse of Michel terme in þe same yere
and by endenture made with þe seyd William Porte etc.

[1] This paragraph has been added in a later hand.

Plate XIII   Cartulary of Chertsey Abbey   15th cent
                                 (E. 164/25, fo. 25v)

Bastard hand

de quibus victum suum acquirere[1] et habere deberent propter raritatem[1] serviencium et
carenciam[1] cultorum et ex hominum epidemeis seu pestilenciis precedentibus sterilis maneat
et inculta, ac domibus et edificiis ad dictum monasterium pertinentibus ipsorumque ecclesia
ob tempestates validas plus solito contingentes ruina absque eorum culpa seu necligencia
collapsis, redditus possessionum de quibus dictum monasterium dotatum extitit ab antiquo
adeo sunt tenues et exiles quod ad hujusmodi edificiorum ac ecclesie reperacionem [*sic*]
et refeccionem ac sustentacionem monachorum juxta numerum a fundacione ejusdem monasterii ordinatum et hospitum recepcionem aliaque onera quibus plus solito multipliciter pre-
gravantur non sufficiunt supportanda.   Sunt eciam ere aliena [*sic*] intanto depressi quod
de bonis dicti monasterii existentibus ad solucionem ejusdem efficiuntur quodammodo
non solvendo, sicque miseria et inopia sunt fatigati quod oportebit predictum conventum
ipsius monasterii contra honestatem religionis et divinum officium in eodem monasterio
fieri consuetum [et pro quo ipsum monasterium extitit fundatum in magna parte dimit-
tere . . .]

[1] The small initial, inserted as a guide to the letterer responsible for the ornamental capitals, is still
visible.

Plate XIV (a)   Remission of Court   1480
                      (Remissions of Court, under arrangement)

Chancery hand

Excellentissimo principi domino Edwardo Dei gracia regi Anglie et Francie et domino
Hibernie Johannes Shirley armiger salutem in eo per quem reges regnant et principes

dominantur. Quia Ricardus Bentley in curia vestra coram justiciariis vestris de banco per breve vestrum de recto Johannem Foune filium Johannis Foune de duobus mesuagiis uno tofto ducentis acris terre viginti acris prati et viginti acris pasture cum pertinenciis in Holyngton', que de me tenet, mea licencia mediante implacitare proponit, vestre celcitudini regie tenore presencium significo curiam meam vobis inde in hac vice remisisse, salvo michi alias jure dominii mei in casu consimili cum acciderit. In cujus rei testimonium has litteras meas fieri feci patentes. Date[1] apud villam Westmonasterii primo die Octobris anno regni vestri vicesimo.

[1] This extension of the abbreviation *Dat'* presumes agreement with *littere*, understood. But the neuter, singular or plural, can also be defended.

Plate XIV (b)   Private Correspondence   1480
                              (S.C. 1/46/242)

Fifteenth-century correspondence hand

Ryȝht worschypfull and to me synguler good lady, I recommende me unto yow, prayng yow[1] to sende me a buck a Wedynsday nexte commyng acordyng to þe promysse þat my master and ye made at my laste beyng with yow, for a specyall frende of myn schall be maryde on Thursday nexte commyng, to þe wyche I have promysyde a buck ; wherfor I pray yow þat he be not dispoyntyde ; and my service schall be þe more redyer to yow at all tymys with þe grace of God, wyche have yow in kepyng. Wryttyn in haste þe xviij. day of Jule.

By yowr servant
William Goldwyn.

Madam, I pray yow to speck to my master for þe xvj. *li.* þat ys dew unto me.

[1] *þat* struck out.

Plate XV (a)   Signification of Excommunication   1493
                              (C. 85/64/2)

Humanistic hand

Excellentissimo in Christo principi et domino, domino Henrico Dei gracia regi Anglie et Francie ac domino Hibernie illustrissimo Willelmus permissione divina Coventrensis et Lich' episcopus salutem in eo per quem reges regnant et principes dominantur. Celsitudini vestre regie patefacimus per presentes quod religiosus vir Simon abbas monasterii Sancte Werburge Cestrie nostre diocesis propter suas manifestas et excrescentes contumacias rebelliones pariter et offensas in non subeundo visitacionem nostram ordinariam, ad quam subeundam certis die et loco autoritate nostra legitime premonitus fuerat, per nos et autoritate nostra ordinaria fuit et est canonice excominicatus et pro tali palam et puplice denunciatus ; in qua quidem excominicacione per quadraginta dies et amplius perseveravit prout adhuc perseverat animo pertinaciter indurato, claves sancte matris ecclesie nequiter [contempnendo . . .]

Plate XV (b)   Foot of Fine   1508
(C.P. 25(1)/232/79)

Common-law hand

C Y R O G R A P H U M[1]

Hec est finalis concordia facta in curia domini regis apud Westmonasterium a die Pasche in unum mensem anno regnorum Henrici regis Anglie et Francie septimi a conquestu vicesimo tercio coram Roberto Rede Johanne Fyssher' Johanne Kyngesmyll' et Johanne Boteler justiciariis et aliis domini regis fidelibus tunc ibi presentibus inter Thomam Best Johannem Best Johannem Ravelyn' et Ricardum Derby querentes et Willelmum Kebyll' et Elizabetham uxorem ejus deforciantes de uno mesuagio uno gardino et una acra terre cum pertinenciis in Hogmore in parochia de Wandelesworth', unde placitum convencionis summonitum fuit inter eos in eadem curia, scilicet quod predicti Willelmus et Elizabetha recognoverunt predicta tenementa cum pertinenciis esse jus ipsius Thome et illa remiserunt et quietaclamaverunt de ipsis Willelmo et Elizabetha et heredibus ipsius Elizabethe predictis Thome Johanni Johanni et Ricardo et heredibus ipsius Thome imperpetuum. Et pro hac recognicione remissione quietaclamancia fine et concordia iidem Thomas Johannes Johannes et Ricardus dederunt predictis Willelmo et Elizabethe viginti libras sterlingorum.

[Surr']

[1] The lower half of this (abbreviated) word appears along the indented edge of the upper margin. See note 1 to Plate III (a) above.

Plate XVI   Letter to a Cambridge Don   1525
(S.P. 1/34, fo. 186)

Free bastard hand

Maister Golde, in the hartyest wyse I can [I] recommend me unto yow, and evyn so thanke yow for the greate labur and peyn that ye take with my chylde, preying yow of your good contynewaunce of the same, and itt myght please yow to cause hym[1] to kepe hys geyre cleyndly and that he may use hym selff lowlie and gently[2] to every man and that ye wyll cause hym to wrytte aftur your hande, for I lyke that hand better then the romayn hand.[3] And as for other thynges concernyng hys larnyng[4] I perceve by your letter that ye order hym better than I can wryte unto yow; wherfore I hooly remytte hym unto yow. And I have send yow for hym for hys comyns and other necessarii[5] thynges xx. *s.* Also my seid son lernyd to syng hys pleyn song, wiche afore he went to gramer scole he colde syng perfettly, and had som insyght in hys prykesong; and therfore I wold prey yow that he myght at convenyant tymes sumwhat use hytt so that he myght not lese all. And any thyng that I can do for yow [6] or [7] any of your fryndes I shall be gladd at all tymes, with the grace of God, who kepe yow. Wrytton at London, the vj. day of Maii, by the handes of all your owne

John Smyth

[1] Written above *theym*, which has been struck through.
[2] The preceding two words are interlined over a caret.
[3] Gold practised two hands, of which examples are reproduced in Plate XVII (a) and (b). The first, used by Gold for writing English, is the hand admired by Smyth; the second, used for Latin, is a humanistic (*i.e.* ' roman ') style.   [4] Written after a false start.
[5] The second *i* seems to have been immediately rubbed out.   [6] *here* struck through.
[7] *f* (beginning *for* ?) struck through.

Plate XVII (a)   Letter from Henry Gold   1534
                               (S.P. 1/82, fo. 151)

Precursor of secretary hand

Honorable, my dutie don to yowr maisterschip after most due maner, so it is that albeit
that yowr mercyfull goodnes is and hath ben mor to me than I am or can be able to
recompense, yeth nature constraynith me (remembryng the greate pitie in yow) humble to
desyer yowr maisterschip in the way of cheritie to have compassion and pitie of my poere
brother ; for of throught[1] he was myserable deceyvede by that false dissembling noune
lyke as I and other wer, and the rather, no dought, by means of the firme credence that I
and other religiouse persons of Syon, Schene and Richmount (whiche he estemede vertuouse
and well lernede) dide gyve onto the saide noune.   His lyving (as yowr maisterschip doith
know) lyeth most by his credence, the whiche taken away, he, his wif and his childern
be in maner but ondon.   Wherfor for Christes passion have compassion of hym and his,
that therby they all may be bownde dayly to pray for you to Gode, whoo ever preserve you[2]
in mercy and in all goodnes.

> [1] *i.e.* ' truth '.   [2] Interlined over a caret.

Plate XVII (b)   Gold's Sermon Notes   *ante* 1534
                               (S.P. 1/83, fo. 149)

Humanistic cursive hand

Math. 19.   Si vis perfectus esse, vade et vende omnia quae habes, et sequere me.
Math. 10.   Nolite possidere aurum neque argentum neque pecuniam in zonis vestris.
Math. 8.   Vulpes[1] foveas habent, et volucres caeli etc.
Math. 17.   Et aparto ore ejus invenies staterem (hoc est duplex didragma), et illum
               sumens da eiis p[ro] me et te.
Actuum 4°.   Dividebant singulis prout cuique opus erat.

> [1] Preceded by *Volucres caeli nidos*, which has been struck through.

Plate XVIII   Enrolled Chancery Decree   1562
                               (C. 78/19, m. 8)

Chancery hand

To have and to holde the said rectorie and parsonage together with all other the premisses
with the appertenaunces[1] unto the said Sir Thomas Pope knight his heires and assignes to
the onlie use of the said Sir Thomas Pope his heires and assignes for ever ; by force whereof
the said Sir Thomas Pope was seased of the said rectorie and parsonage and other the
premisses in his demeane as of fee ; and soo beinge thereof quietlie and lawfullie seased,
of a good vertuous and charitable disposicione to the furtherans and encrease of learninge

relife of the poore and thadvancemente of Godes glorie (lycence beinge firste obteaned and gottene of the late most famous princes Quene Marie under her heighnes Greate Seale of England) did fownd and erecte one college in Oxforde within the countie of Oxforde by the name of the college of the most hollye blessed and indevidet Trennytie and did further incorporate the same with the Presidente Fellowes and Schollers of the same college, and furthermore for the better mentenaunce thereof to the use afforesaid did also amongeste other mannors landes tenementes and hereditamentes gyve and graunte the said rectorie and parsonage and all other the premisses with there appertenaunces[2] unto the said Presidente Fellowes and Schollers, to have and to holde to them and to ther successors for ever ; by force whereof the said Presidente Fellowes and Schollers were thereof seased accordingelie and so seased did by there tenauntes and fermors of the premisses of longe time and space quietelie perceave take and enjoye the proffittes thereof cominge and growinge without lett hinderaunce vexacione or trowble of any persone or persones untill of late, that is to say the xx[th] of Auguste last before thexhibitinge of the said bill of compleynte, that the said Lord Riche, myndinge the utter ympoverishemente of the said compleynantes and subvercione of the said vertewouse and godlie fowndacione . . .

[1] The *er* of this word has been indicated twice over : once incorrectly by the use of Sign No. 3 (obliterating an erroneously written superior *a*), and again by the bar across the descender of the second *p*.

[2] Sign No. 3 is here again used incorrectly with *p* to replace suppressed *er*.

Plate XIX (a)   Return of Commissioners administering the Oath of   1579
Supremacy to Justices of the Peace
(S.P. 12/133, No. 11, fo. 4)

Common-law hand

NOMINA JUSTICIARIORUM PACIS QUI ABSENTES FUERUNT

Arthurus Manwarynge miles — Ytt was deposed by hys sonne that his father was sycke.
Georgius Blunt miles — Itt was affyrmed that he was att London att the tyme of thassizes.

Rolandus Haywarde miles
Georgius Bromley attornatus ducatus Lanc'. — Ytt was affyrmed that he was in circuyte in Northwales.

Willelmus Leighton' armiger — He was in his circuyte in Southwales.
Robertus Corbett armiger
Edwardus Graye armiger — Ytt was affyrmed that he was sicke.
Edmundus Cornwall' armiger — Ytt was testyfyed bye hys servaunte that he was sycke.
Thomas Eyton' armiger — Itt was affyrmed that he is impotent.
Edmundus Walter armiger — Itt was affyrmed he was in circuyte in Southwales.
Johannes Horde armiger
Rolandus Lacon' armiger
Thomas Powell' armiger

Plate XIX (b)   Letter to the Council   1586
                                 (S.P. 12/193, No. 50)

Secretary hand

Maye yt please your good Lordshipps to be advertised that, as it lyked your honors to geve
me in comaundment, so have I the xvth of this September with the assystance of Mr. George
Villers apprehended John Palmer of Kegworthe in this countie of Leicester and have sent
him to your honors by my brother Anthonye Cave, I trust under sure custodie.   It was
my happe in my jorney to Kegworthe to find him in his bedd at Lowghboroughe, emongest
other yonge gentelmen at Sir George Hastinges his house, wher they had contynued (for
the moste part) certen daies, recreatinge them selfes in huntinge and hawkinge.   And takinge
him presentlie thence to Kegworthe my selfe and Mr Villers searched his chambers and
studdye and have not found any wrytinges or letters concerninge Her Majestie or the estatte.

Plate XX (a)   Letter to Lord Burghley   1589
                                (S.P. 12/222, No. 23)

Secretary hand

My very good Lord,

     Wheras by my late letters your Lordship was advertised of Hir Majesties pleasure
for the respiting of the repaire of the souldiours appointed to be levied in those counties
unto London from the xxth of this moneth untill the 25th, thease are now to signifie unto
your Lordship that for some great considerations it is thought meete by Hir Highnes that
the same should be againe deferred from the saied xxvth day untill the first of February.
And therefore hir pleasure is that accordingly you give order for the stay . . .

Plate XX (b)   Chancery (Crown Office) Precedent Book   *c.* 1610
                            (C. 193/6, No. 207 p. 1)

Engrossing secretary hand

In default whereof the rogues and vagabondes have of late yeares growne bolde and mul-
tiplied to a greater nomber then the common wealth can suffer ; wee therefore mindinge
to have due reformacion herein and to have the contentes of the said statute dulie performed,
trustinge in your approved fidelities wisdomes and circumspeccions, have authorised
assigned and appointed you to be our commissioners, and by theis presentes doe give unto
you or anie three or more of you full power and authoritie from tyme to time hereafter
to inquire aswell by the oathes of good and lawfull men of the said countie of A. as by the
examinacion of witnesses or the parties themselves or by anie other good and lawfull waies
or meanes whatsoever whereby the truth may best be found out what somes of money or
other thinges have byn collected or gathered within the said countie for or towardes the
ereccion of anie house or houses of correccion or anie stockes or other thinges to sett poore
on worke or for the maintenaunce thereof at anie [tyme . . .]

H.E.D—H

Plate XXI (a)   Pipe Roll   1628
(E. 372/473, *Civitas Norwic'*)

Pipe Office hand

[Iidem vicecomites . . . reddunt compotum de . . . liiij. solidis] iiij. denariis pro civibus et ballivis civitatis Norwic' ibidem Et xl. solidis pro eisdem [civibus ibidem Et. x. solidis pro Johanne Mannynger ibidem] Et xij. libris xvj. solidis ij. denariis de pluribus debitis ibidem. Summa cxlij. libre v[ij. solidi v. denarii.   In thesauro iiij. libre xxxj^{mo} Octobris anno quarto] per dictos vicecomites de exitibus ballive sue Et in thesauro c. libre in duabus talliis de [quibus onerantur supra infra quandam summam] cxiij. librarum viij. solidorum sub nomine civium Norwic' de feodi firma ville sue pro [guarderoba domini Regis Et in thesauro xiiij. libre xix. solidi v. denarii] xxix^{no} Novembris anno quarto de firmis et aliis debitis per dictos vicecomites de [remanencia compoti sui de solucione Et domine Marie Henriette Regine] Anglie Scocie Francie et Hibernie consorti Regis cui Rex per litteras suas patentes sub magno sigillo suo Anglie [gerentes datam xiiij^{to} die Marcii anno regni sui Anglie Scocie Francie et Hibernie] secundo dedit concessit et assignavit annualem redditum viginti trium librarum et octo solidorum durante vita n[aturali xxiij. libre viij. solidi . . .]

Plate XXI (b)   Minute Book of Commissioners   1635
to inquire into Fees of Courts
(E. 315/329, fo. 39)

' *Mixed* ' hand

Upon consideracion taken this day of the small letter written[1] in entring the pleadings in the courts at the common lawe and of the secretary hand in the English courts[2] mixed with the Italian hand, which is conceived will in short tyme[3] weare and become illegible, that it bee certified by the commissioners in some fitt place upon their next certificates of the officers of those courts to His Majesty[4] as deservinge reformacion.

         [1] *somety* (beginning *sometymes*) struck through.
         [2] That is, the courts using the English language.
         [3] *will* struck through.   [4] *that* struck through

Plate XXII   Lord Treasurer's Remembrancer's Memoranda Roll   1633
(E. 368/629, rot. 152(2))

L.T.R. hand

[Inquisicio . . . capta . . . per sacramentum . . . proborum et legalium hominum de] comitatu predicto Qui dicunt super sacramentum suum predictum quod Gracia Babthorpe nuper de Osgodby in parochia de Hemingbroughe in comitatu Ebor' vidua in cedula commissioni huic[1] annexata nominata die conviccionis sue vel postea seisita fuit in nomine juncture[2] sue pro termino vite ipsius Gracie de et in manerio de Osgodby cum pertinenciis ac de et in tribus mesuagiis centum acris terre arrabilis prati pascue[3] et pasture cum pertinenciis in Osgodby annui valoris in omnibus exitibus ultra reprisas decem librarum unde due partes dicto domino regi annui valoris in omnibus exitibus ultra reprisas sex librarum tresdecim solidorum et quatuor denariorum[4] In cujus rei testimonium tam commissionarii predicti quam juratores predicti sigillis suis [*sic*] die et anno predictis apposuerunt.   Petit etiam idem Guido Palmes miles auditum predicte inquisicionis indentate capte apud pre-dictum[5] castrum Ebor' predicto vicesimo octavo die Septembris dicto anno regni dicti domini Regis nunc Caroli secundo, et ei similiter legitur in hec verba : Inquisicio indentata capta apud castrum Ebor' in comitatu [Ebor' . . .]

[1] This word has been inserted by way of amendment at the end of the line, where there was room for it, but it should properly have preceded *commissioni*.
[2] This is undoubtedly the word intended, but the scribe's attempt to retrieve a false start has made the actual manuscript reading uncertain.
[3] Inserted over a caret.
[4] Sc. *pertinent*, or some such verb.   [5] Interlined over a caret.

Plate XXIII   King's Remembrancer's Memoranda Roll   1642
                       (E. 159/482, Trinity Communia, rot. 15)

K.R. hand

Adhuc de tenore decreti inter Edwardum dominum Herbert et Edwardum dominum Mountague querentes et Philippum Clement et alios defendentes incipientis in ventre rotuli precedentis.

freely grynd theire corne grayne and malt at the sayd mills and further sett forth that they did nott knowe that all the tenauntes and inhabitantes of the sayd towne of Oundle of right and ancient usage ought to grynd all theire corne grayne and malt which they spent in theire sayd howses at the sayd mills and that they did verely beleive that the sayd water mills of Oundle weare not sufficient and able to grynd all the corne grayne and malt which was spent by the sayd inhabitantes of Oundle

Plate XXIV   Petition to the Privy Council   1640
                       (S.P. 16/454, fo. 68)

The petition itself is in a ' mixed ' hand, with displayed matter in a more or less pure italic ; the Council's decision, which is underwritten, is in a cognate italic.

To the Right Honourable the Lordes and others
of His Majestys most honourable Privy Councell.

The humble peticion of Richard Beaumont
apprentice unto James James an apothecary, London,

Humbly sheweth
That your peticioner was sent for by warrant from the Right Honourable Sir Francis Windebanke knight Principall Secretary of State and thereupon was examyned by his honour for speaking some unadvised wordes, which hee did not deny ; and upon report

to your Lordshipps of your peticioners humble confession, hee was justly comitted by your honours to the prison of the Fleete.

> Your peticioner most humbly beseecheth your Lordshipps, in regard that hee is heartily sorry that ever hee spake such wordes, and doth purpose never to offend in the like kinde, that your honours out of your accustomed clemency wilbee pleased to give order for his enlargement. And your peticioner will pray etc.

At the Court at Whitehall the 20th of May 1640

Mr. Secretary Windebanke is prayed to consider of this peticion and to take such order therein as with the advise of Mr. Attorney Generall hee shall thinck good.

Edw. Nicholas

Plate XXV	Ecclesiastical Cause Paper	1671

(Borthwick Institute, York, R. VII. H. 2973)

Late 'mixed' hand

effectum revocat et subducit, eandemque sic revocandam et subducendam fore decerni petiit,[1] et ulterius allegavit that allthough by ye custome of ye said parish of Manchester in ye said libell deduced and confessed by ye party of ye said Ralph Bibby in ye former instance of this cause, every parishoner-householder havinge a house and family within ye said parish of Manchester hath paid or ought to have paid to ye owners proprietaryes possessours or farmours of ye rectory tythes or other ecclesia[sti]call rights or to his or theire use att ye feast of Easter yearly, foure pence for oblacions of himselfe and wife, and mother two pence, for house one penny, for garden a halfe penny, for a farrowe cow one penny, for a cow and a calfe penny halfe penny, for hay one penny of currant English money accordinge to ye said custome, yet he ye said Ralph Bibby was not a parishoner-householder, nor had or kept an house or family within ye said parish of Manchester, ye monthes or yeares libellate

[1] About a line and a half obliterated here.

Plate XXVI	Recovery Roll	1682

(C.P. 43/396, rot. 143)

Common-law hand

Et predictus Willelmus in propria persona sua venit et defendit jus suum quando etc., et vocat inde ad warantum Johannem Hawtyn seniorem generosum, qui presens est hic in curia in propria persona sua et gratis tenementa et communiam predicta cum pertinenciis ei warantizat etc. Et super hoc predictus Jeremias petit versus ipsum Johannem tenentem per waranciam suam tenementa et communiam predicta cum pertinenciis in forma predicta etc. ; et unde dicit quod ipsemet fuit seisitus de tenementis et communia predictis cum pertinenciis in dominico suo ut de feodo et jure tempore pacis tempore domini Regis nunc, capiendo inde explesias ad valenciam etc., et in que etc. ; et inde producit sectam etc.

| Plate XXVII | Petition for Reprieve | 1682 |
| | (S.P. 29/418) | |

The petition is in a late ' mixed' hand, with displayed matter in italic ; the underwritten minute in a sloped ' mixed' hand.

[no other] person being present, shee was unfortunately found guilty of murther according to the severity of the laws of this kingdome, and is adjudged to be executed in the city of Oxford on Thursday next.

Now inasmuch as your petic[i]oner is greatly sorrowfull for her sin, and much more for the losse of her child and not fitt to dye, being distracted in mind,

> Therefore your poore petic[i]oner humbly implores Your Majesties mercy in your generall pardon and your gratious repreive from execucion untill the said pardon will issue forth.
> And your petic[i]oner as in duty bound shall pray etc.

Earle of Clarendon received some deposicions upon oath and moved ye King ; Mr. Justice Warcup from his lordship gott a reprieve which was signed 24 January and delivered to [a] person yat came expresse from Oxford.

| Plate XXVIII | Coroner's Inquisition | 1729 |
| | (Q.B. 11/29, Michaelmas 1729) | |

Engrossing hand

[*Som'*.] Inquisitio indentata capta apud Stafford infra parochiam de Barwick in comitatu praedicto[1] coram me Georgio Cary generoso uno coronatorum domini Regis in et pro comitatu praedicto super visum corporis cujusdam Hannae Griffen de Stafford praedicta ibidem mortui jacentis per sacramentum Willelmi Bulpin Georgii Moore Johannis Pexford Johannis Highmoore Willelmi Willmington Johannis Grange Georgii Chapman Geórgii Foon Willelmi Harris Giles Budghill Johannis Higgins Johannis Ring Samuelis Bartlet proborum et legalium hominum juratorum triatorum et oneratorum ad inquirendum qualiter et quomodo praedicta Hanna Griffen ad mortem suam devenit ; qui dicunt super sacramentum suum quod praedicta Hanna primo die Julii anno regni domini nostri Georgii secundi nunc Magnae Britanniae etc. Regis secundo apud Stafford praedictam ex visitatione Dei obiit et non aliter ad eorum notitiam. In cujus rei testimonium tam ego praefatus coronator quam juratores praedicti huic inquisitioni sigilla nostra alternatim apposuimus die anno loco supradictis [*sic*].

Geo. Cary coronator
(Seal)

[1] The date of the inquisition, which should have been stated here, has been omitted.

Plate XXIX   Proceedings in the King's Bench   1733
                              (Q.B. 28/124, rot. 1 (2))

Common-law hand (ll. 1–11) and engrossing hand (from l. 11)[1]

[Quod quidem indictamentum dictus dominus Rex] nunc coram se postea certis de causis venire fecit terminandum etc. ; per quod preceptum est vicecomiti comitatus Midd'x' predicti quod non omittat etc. quin venire faciat eum ad respondendum etc.   Et modo, scilicet die Martis proxima post[2] octabas Sancti Hillarii isto eodem termino coram dicto ∣domino Rege apud Westmonasterium venit predictus Josephus Whittorn alias Whithorn per Henricum Masterman attornatum suum et habito auditu indictamenti predicti dicit quod ipse non est inde culpabilis ; et de hoc ponit se super patriam ; et Willelmus Bellamy armiger coronator et attornatus dicti domini Regis nunc in curia ipsius Regis coram ipso Rege, qui pro eodem domino Rege in hac parte sequitur, similiter etc.   Ideo veniat inde jurata coram dicto domino Rege a die Pasche in quindecim dies ubicunque etc., per quos etc., et qui etc., ad recognoscendum etc., quia tam etc.   Idem dies datus est tam prefato Willelmo Bellamy armigero, qui sequitur etc., quam predicto Josepho Whittorn alias Whithorn etc.   At which day before the lord the King at Westminster came as well James Burrow esquire the present coroner and attorney of the said lord the King in the court of the said lord the King before the King himself, who prosecutes for the King in this behalf, as the said Joseph Whittorn otherwise Whithorn by [his attorney . . .]

    [1] These proceedings straddle the date (25 March 1733) on which the Act 4 Geo. II, c. 26, came into force (see above, p. 23).   The record was begun, in Hilary term, in Latin and the common-law hand, and resumed in Easter term in English and the engrossing hand.
    [2] Interlined over a caret.

Plate XXX (a)   Parliament Roll   1760
                                 (C. 65/739, m. 2)

Chancery hand

[Le] Roy le veult.[1]

    An Act for amending and widening the road leading from the town of Falmouth in the county of Cornwall through the towns of Penrin Helston and[2] Marazion and from thence to and over Marazion river and bridge and two hundred feet to the westward of the said river and bridge.

    [1] Conclusion of the next preceding Act enrolled.   [2] Interlined over a caret.

Plate XXX (b)   Parliament Roll   1859
                                 (C. 65/5096, p. 427)

Chancery hand

Cui quidem Bille in se formam Actus continenti prelecte et ad plenum intellecte per̄ dictam dominam Reginam ex authoritate Parliamenti sic responsum est.

                                                    La Reine le veult.

Plate XXXI   Deed Enrolled in Chancery   1830
                              (C. 54/10764, m. 40)

Engrossing hand

[All that the said cha]pel or building and the land or ground thereunto belonging, situate lying and being in the town of Llanelly in the county of Carmarthen, containing in the whole by common estimation forty two square yards or thereabouts, be the same mor[e] or less, which said premises are more particularly delineated and described in the ground plan thereof drawn in the margin of these presents ; together with all ways paths passages lights easements waters watercourses privileges profits commodities advantages and appurtenances to the said hereditaments and premises belonging or in [anywise appertaining ; t]o have and to hold . . .

Plate XXXII   Monumental Inscription of Lora, Viscountess Downe   1836
                            (York Minster)

The lettering of this inscription is reproduced here in order to illustrate the point made on p. 26 above, that a check is imposed on reading when the reader is unable to identify whole words at a glance. It is doubtful whether any reader will have so much difficulty with the gothic lettering of the verses as to need a transcript ; but those who find themselves obliged to spell out the first line letter by letter will probably also find that their facility increases with every line successfully read.

TABLE OF CONFUSIBILIA

The purpose of this list of potential resemblances between letters is to suggest, to the apprentice reader of manuscript, possible alternatives to his own first impressions. It is, of course, for him to decide whether the resemblance suggested actually occurs in the document before him. The numbers in brackets indicate the centuries in which confusion may be easy.

A	(13) D.	N	(13) H.
a	(single-bowled) (13) ci.		(cabriole-legged) (14) ligature of
	(single-bowled, in final position)		long s and t or c.
	(13) o.	n	*See* the remarks on minims on
	(double-bowled) (13) ligature of ct.		p. 27.
B	(14) G, H.	O	(13–15) E.
b	(13–15) v.	o	(14–16) reversed e.
bb	(in ligature) (13) lb.		(in final position) (13) a.
C	(12, 13) G.	p	(12) *thorn*; (15–17) x.
c	(before 15) t ; (most dates) e.	q	(13) Abbreviation Sign No. 6.
ci	*See* a.	R	(most dates) K.
ct	(in ligature). *See* a.	r	(tailed Arabic-2 type) (14) z,
D	(13) A.		*yogh.*
d	(15 onwards) reversed e.	S	(beaver-tailed) (late 13) M.
E	(13–15) O.	s	(long) (all dates) f : (in ligature).
e	(most dates) c.		*See* N.
	(reversed) (14–16) o ; (15 onwards)		(short) (14) g.
	d.	t	(before 15) c.
f	(all dates) long s.	u, v	*See* the remarks on minims on
G	(12, 13) C ; (14) B.		p. 27.
g	(early 14) s ; (15) x.	v	(13–15) b.
H	(13) N ; (14) B.	w	(13–15) lk.
i, j	*See* the remarks on minims on	x	(14) y ; (15) g ; (15–17) p.
	p. 27.	y	(14) x. *See also* the remarks on
K	(most dates) R.		*thorn* on p. 39.
lb	(13) ligature of bb.	z	(14). *See* r.
lk	(13–15) w.	yogh	(14). *See* r.
M	*See* S.	Abbrevi-	
m	*See* the remarks on minims on	ation	
	p. 27.	Sign 6.	(13) q.

BIBLIOGRAPHY

I. General

(The works marked * contain transcribed facsimiles)

G. Battelli : *Lezioni di Paleografia (3rd ed. ; Vatican, 1949).

N. Denholm-Young : Handwriting in England and Wales (Cardiff, 1954). (Transcripts of six of the thirty-one plates.)

Hilary Jenkinson : *The Later Court Hands in England (Cambridge, 1927).

Charles Johnson and Hilary Jenkinson : *English Court Hand, 1066–1500 (Oxford, 1915).

E. A. Lowe : ' Handwriting ' in The Legacy of the Middle Ages, edd. C. G. Crump and E. F. Jacob (Oxford, 1926).

F. Madan : Books in Manuscript (1920).

M. Prou : *Manuel de paléographie latine et française (4th ed. ; Paris, 1924).

F. Steffens : *Lateinische Paläographie (2nd ed. ; Fribourg, 1907 ; French ed. Paris and Trèves, 1908–10).

E. Maunde Thompson : *Introduction to Greek and Latin Palaeography (Oxford, 1912).

L. Traube : Vorlesungen und Abhandlung (Munich, 1909–20).

II. Materials and Instruments

C. M. Briquet : Les Filigranes (Paris, 1907).

P. M. Caneparius : De Atramentis (1660).

R. B. Haselden : Scientific Aids for the Study of Manuscripts (Bibliographical Society, 1935).

E. Heawood : Papers used in England after 1600 (1931).

—— : ' Further Notes on Papers used in England after 1600 ' in The Library, Ser. V, Vol. II (1947).

—— : ' The Use of Watermarks in Dating old Maps and Documents ', in the Geographical Journal, May, 1924.

D. Hunter : Papermaking (1947).

C. A. Mitchell : Documents and their Scientific Examination (2nd ed., 1935).

D. V. Thompson : The Materials of Mediaeval Painting (1936).

III. Languages

(a) Latin

J. H. Baxter and Charles Johnson : Medieval Latin Word-List (Oxford, 1934 ; re-issued 1947).

Charles du Fresne, seigneur Du Cange : Glossarium Mediae et Infimae Latinitatis (numerous editions).

H. V. P. Nunn : Introduction to Ecclesiastical Latin (1922).

W. E. Plater and H. J. White : Grammar of the Vulgate (Oxford, 1926).

K. Strecker : Introduction à l'étude du latin médiéval (Paris, 1946).

(b) Anglo-Norman French

F. Godefroy : Dictionnaire de l'ancienne langue française (Paris, 1881–1902 ; reprinted 1938).

R. Kelham : Anglo-Norman Dictionary (1779).

F. W. Maitland : Year Books 1 and 2 Edward II (Selden Society XVII) (1903) ; introduction on the Anglo-French language. See also the introductions to Selden Society LII (1934) and LIV (1935).

M. K. Pope : From Latin to Modern French (Manchester, 1934).

IV. Transcribed Facsimiles

(See also the works marked * in I. General above)

P. S. Allen and H. W. Garrod: *Merton Muniments* (Oxford Historical Society, 1926).

E. A. Bond: *Facsimiles of Ancient Charters in the British Museum* (1873–8).

L. Delisle: *Recueil des actes de Henri II, roi d'Angleterre* . . . (Paris, 1908).

H. E. P. Grieve: *Examples of English Handwriting, 1150–1750* (Essex County Council, 1954).

J. Kirchner: *Scriptura Latina Libraria* (Munich, 1955).

New Palaeographical Society, Publications, 1903–30.

Palaeographical Society, Publications, 1873–1901.

H. E. Salter: *Oxford Charters* (Oxford, 1929).

W. B. Sanders: *Facsimiles of National Manuscripts, England* (1865–9).

F. M. Stenton: *Facsimiles of Early Northamptonshire Charters* (Northamptonshire Record Society, 1930).

G. F. Warner and H. J. Ellis: *Facsimiles of Royal and other Charters in the British Museum* (1903).

V. Abbreviation

A. Cappelli: *Dizionario delle abbreviature latine ed italiane* (3rd ed.; Milan, 1929; reprinted 1949).

L. A. Chassant: *Dictionnaire des abréviations latines et françaises* (7th ed.; Paris, 1884).

Sir T. D. Hardy: *Registrum Palatinum Dunelmense*, Vol. IV (1878); Introduction.

C. T. Martin: *The Record Interpreter* (2nd ed.; 1910).

L. Traube: *Nomina Sacra* (Munich, 1907).

VI. Publications in Record Type

Publications of the Record Commissioners, such as *Nonarum Inquisitiones* (ed. G. Vanderzee, 1807); *Abbreviatio Placitorum* (ed. Rt. Hon G. Rose and W. Illingworth, 1811); *Statutes of the Realm* (ed. A. Luders and others, 1810–28); *Rotuli Scotiae* (ed. D. Macpherson and others, 1814–19); *Rotuli Litterarum Clausarum* (ed. T. D. Hardy; 1833–44); *Proceedings of the Privy Council of England* (ed. Sir N. H. Nicolas, 1834–7); *Rotuli Litterarum Patentium* (ed. T. D. Hardy, 1835); *Rotuli Curiae Regis* (ed. Sir F. Palgrave, 1835); *Fines sive Pedes Finium* (ed. J. Hunter, 1835–44); *Documents Illustrative of English History in the 13th and 14th Centuries* . . . (ed. H. Cole, 1844).

Publications of the Pipe Roll Society issued before 1904.

W. Paley Baildon: *Select Civil Pleas*, Vol. I, 1200–3 (Selden Society, III) (1889).

VII. Miscellaneous

G. F. Hill: *The Development of Arabic Numerals in Europe* (Oxford, 1915).

Hilary Jenkinson: 'The Use of Arabic and Roman Numerals in English Archives' in *Antiquaries Journal*, Vol. VI (1926).

——: 'Notes on the Study of Punctuation of the Sixteenth Century' in *Review of English Studies*, Vol. III (1926).

R. L. Marshall: *The Historical Criticism of Documents* (S.P.C.K. Helps for Students of History, 1920).

R. Steele (ed.): *The Earliest Arithmetics in English* (Early English Text Society, Extra Series, CXVIII, 1922).

E. Vinaver: 'Principles of Textual Emendation' in *Studies . . . presented to Prof. M. K. Pope* (Manchester, 1939).

INDEX